The CONFEDERATE CHEROKEES

The
CONFEDERATE
CHEROKEES

John Drew's Regiment of Mounted Rifles

W. Craig Gaines

Louisiana State University Press
Baton Rouge and London

Designer: Sylvia Malik Loftin
Typeface: Palatino
Typesetter: The Composing Room of Michigan, Inc.

The author gratefully acknowledges the Thomas Gilcrease Institute of American History and Art, Tulsa, Oklahoma, for permission to quote from the Grant Foreman Papers, the John Ross Papers, the John Drew Papers, and the William P. Ross Papers; the National Park Service at Pea Ridge National Military Park for permission to quote from "The Indians at Pea Ridge," by Edwin C. Bearss; the Western History Collections of the University of Oklahoma for permission to quote from the Cherokee Nation Papers, Cate Collection; and the Oklahoma Historical Society for permission to quote from Joseph Thoburn (ed.), "The Cherokee Question," *Chronicles of Oklahoma*, II (March, 1924), 141–252, and Dean Trickett, "The Civil War in the Indian Territory, 1862," *Chronicles of Oklahoma*, XIX (December, 1941), 381–96. Passages from *Reluctant General: The Life and Times of Albert Pike*, by Robert Lipscomb Duncan, are copyright © 1961 by Robert Lipscomb Duncan and are reprinted by permission of John Hawkins & Associates, Inc., 71 W. 23rd St., NYC 10010.

Library of Congress Cataloging-in-Publication Data

Gaines, W. Craig, 1953–
   The Confederate Cherokees: John Drew's regiment of mounted rifles
/ W. Craig Gaines.
     p.   cm.
   Bibliography: p.
   Includes index.
   ISBN 0-8071-1488-X (alk. paper)
   1. Cherokee Indians—History—Civil War, 1861–1865.
2. Confederate States of America. Army. Arkansas Cherokee Mounted Rifles, 1st. 3. Indians of North America—History—Civil War, 1861–1865. 4. United States—History—Civil War, 1861–1865—Regimental histories. 5. United States—History—Civil War, 1861–1865—Participation, Indian. I. Title.
E99.C5G16 1989
973.7'467—dc19   88-31358
                                               CIP

To my wife, Arla, who has endured my long and labored efforts in completing this project

Contents

Illustrations

Preface

A wide variety of sources must be researched and analyzed when writing on a historical event long after all the participants have died. This book tells of the events that affected a Cherokee Indian regiment and the Cherokee Nation during the American Civil War. Finding information concerning century-old events is difficult enough, but since many of the people concerned with the events were Cherokees who barely spoke English, I had to rely on accounts derived from generally mixed-blood officers and leaders of the Cherokee Nation who spoke and wrote both English and Cherokee, as well as reports by white Confederate and Union officers. As is common in any Indian history, the viewpoint of the full-bloods has not been well documented, so I have often only alluded to it.

I am indebted to the late Grant Foreman for compiling so much information on Drew's regiment, Chief John Ross, and John Drew. Also, I wish to thank the Thomas Gilcrease Institute of American History and Art, the Oklahoma Historical Society, the University of Oklahoma, the National Archives, Northeastern State University, and the University of Tulsa for information vital to the telling of this story. The cooperation and assistance of the staffs of these institutions are greatly appreciated.

Although this is primarily a history of a Confederate Cherokee regiment supporting the Ross political party during the Civil War, it is also a story of individual Cherokees and the complex issues of their time. I have provided some background information necessary to understand individual decisions of the members of Drew's Cherokee regiment. In history we too often remember dates and events rather than the human factors behind the events. For the Cherokees, relationships and human emotions are the key ingredients, or catalysts, in the destruction that spread among them in 1861 and 1862. I hope this work will both enlighten and inform readers of the strange circumstances that divided and almost destroyed a nation of Indians during the Civil War.

The CONFEDERATE CHEROKEES

1
The Neutral Cherokee Nation

In 1859, on the eve of the American Civil War, the Cherokee Nation, in what is now the northeastern part of the state of Oklahoma, had a total population of almost twenty-two thousand. Of this number, only about four thousand male Cherokees were citizens or eligible to vote. The rest of the population consisted of about four thousand Negroes (mostly slaves but a few freedmen), about a thousand whites, and Cherokee women and children or non-Cherokee Indians. About fifteen hundred Cherokee students attended thirty public schools in which all but two of the teachers were Cherokees.[1]

By heritage the Cherokees were generally Southerners, having grown up under the system of Negro slavery on plantations and small farms. Before being forced from their ancestral homelands in Alabama, Georgia, North Carolina, Kentucky, and Tennessee, the Cherokees lived in villages as bands of hunters and farmers that united for mutual protection. Among their neighbors were the Creeks, Choctaws, and Chickasaws.

The arrival of the Europeans and the colonization of the eastern American seaboard encroached upon the Cherokee homeland. Northern missionaries and southern traders intermarried into the Cherokee tribe, bringing great changes in the traditional attitudes and polarizations among different groups within the tribe. Some Cherokees preferred the old ways and distrusted the land-hungry white man; others wanted progress and urged adoption of many of the white man's ways to improve the Cherokee standard of living.

As several generations passed, the mixed-blood Cherokees began to take control of tribal affairs, and fewer full-bloods remained in positions of power. The mixed-bloods were often in business with white traders and got lucrative government and tribal contracts, increasing their influence in the tribe. Tribal members became edu-

1. Emitt Starr, *History of the Cherokee Indians and Their Legends and Folklore* (Oklahoma City, 1921), 261.

cated in missionary schools and some went to colleges in the North, where a few met and married educated white women.

Many Cherokees, along with Creeks and Choctaws, fought against the pro-British "Red Stick" Creeks in the Red Stick War during the War of 1812. The Red Sticks were involved in both a civil war against neutral and pro–United States Creeks and a war against the Americans. On August 30, 1813, a group of Red Sticks led by William Weatherford, also known as Red Eagle, who was seven-eighths white and one-eighth Creek, killed 367 whites, Indians, and Negroes in Fort Mims, the fortified residence of Samuel Mims, a mixed-blood Creek. Some 600 Cherokees, mostly mixed-bloods, organized into nineteen companies and helped the Americans, led by Major General Andrew Jackson, destroy the Red Stick Creeks in a series of battles, culminating at a horseshoe bend of the Tallapoosa River, where the Cherokees lost 18 killed and 35 wounded out of a total of 49 killed and 157 wounded in General Jackson's force and the Red Sticks lost over 800 killed.[2]

Following the American victory over the Red Sticks, the influence of the United States, under Jackson's leadership and expansionist policies, brought civilization to the Cherokees and other Indian tribes. The Cherokees had their own alphabet created in 1821 by mixed-blood George Guess or Sequoyah. Within a few years almost one-half of the Cherokee men could read and write in their native language. Missionaries printed Bibles and psalm books in Cherokee and converted most of the tribe to Christianity. In 1828 the *Cherokee Phoenix* was established as a native-language newspaper, enabling Cherokees to learn of local, national, and international events.[3]

American settlers on the boundaries of the lands of the Cherokees and other Indian tribes in the Southeast put political and economic pressure on the state and federal governments to remove Indians to the West and allow white settlement on Indian lands in the Southeast. Some Cherokees, who became known as the Old Settlers or Western Cherokees, emigrated voluntarily to Indian Territory. A few settled in the Mexican province of Texas, which later became the Republic of Texas. The Cherokees never seriously considered resist-

2. Kenny A. Franks, *Stand Watie and the Agony of the Cherokee Nation* (Memphis, 1979), 3; Gary E. Moulton, *John Ross, Cherokee Chief* (Athens, Ga., 1978), 12; and Marquis James, *The Life of Andrew Jackson* (Indianapolis, 1938), 156–57.
3. Morris L. Wardell, *A Political History of the Cherokee Nation, 1838–1907* (Norman, 1977), 4.

ing the Americans with force. The Red Stick War had convinced them that they could not possibly win an armed conflict against the more numerous and better-armed Americans.

Internal Cherokee politics and family relations divided the tribe into several factions. The Cherokee Ridge party or Treaty party, headed by Major John Ridge, also called the Ridge, wanted a treaty with the United States to obtain new lands in the West to which to emigrate. The Ridge party had the support of many mixed-bloods. The Ross party was led by Chief John Ross, who was seven-eighths white and one-eighth Cherokee and was the elected leader of the Cherokee Nation. John Ross was born in Rossville, Georgia, on October 3, 1790. His first act of public service was in 1809, when the Cherokee Indian agent Colonel Return J. Meigs sent him on a mission to visit the Cherokees in Arkansas. Ross served as an adjutant under Major Ridge in Andrew Jackson's army during the Red Stick War. In 1817 Ross served in the Cherokee Council's National Committee, in 1827 he was elected president of the Cherokee Constitutional Convention, and in 1828 he was elected chief of the Cherokees east of the Mississippi River. His political party was supported by the full-bloods, but its leaders were mixed-bloods with traditional leanings.[4]

Members of the minority Ridge party led by Major Ridge reluctantly signed the Treaty of New Echota in 1835 and exchanged the ancient Cherokee homelands in Alabama, Georgia, North Carolina, and Tennessee for new lands in Indian Territory without the consent of the rest of the Cherokees. Indian Territory, far from the Cherokee homelands, consisted of what is now the state of Oklahoma.

Strangely enough, in 1807 Major Ridge had been one of a party of five Cherokees that killed Chief Doublehead for signing a treaty in 1806 that ceded Cherokee lands in Tennessee and Kentucky to the United States. Chief Doublehead was bribed to sign the treaty, and he had killed a Cherokee who denounced his treachery. Major Ridge was instrumental in establishing the law that any Cherokee who sold tribal land without the National Council's authorization was a traitor and could be executed.[5]

After the Treaty of New Echota most members of the Ridge party

4. James Mooney, "Myths of the Cherokee," in *Nineteenth Annual Report of the Bureau of American Ethnology to the Secretary of the Smithsonian Institution, 1897–98* (Washington, D.C., 1900), pt. I, pp. 224–25.
5. Grace Steele Woodward, *The Cherokees* (Norman, 1963), 129–30.

voluntarily emigrated to lands in present Oklahoma and Arkansas. Chief John Ross and the Ross party, however, opposed the Treaty of New Echota. The United States, in the classic strategy of divide and conquer, recognized the Treaty of New Echota as binding on all Cherokees, not just the Ridge party, and the Ross party Cherokees were soon forced from their farms and villages by the United States Army and various state militias. The Cherokees traveled by foot, on horses, in wagons, and in boats to Indian Territory.

Many Cherokees fell sick and died during the long forced march, which became known as the Trail of Tears because few families made the trip to their new homes without the loss of at least one loved one. Chief John Ross's wife, Quatie Martin Ross (also called Elizabeth Ross), was among those who died on the trip to Indian Territory. She was buried in 1839 at Little Rock, Arkansas, in a cemetery lot owned by Albert Pike, a lawyer and friend of Chief Ross. Sickness and fatigue almost wiped out some families. Some Cherokees stayed behind in their ancestral homeland, hiding out in the hills, and became known as the Eastern Cherokees.

The Ross party considered Major Ridge and the other leaders of the Ridge party to be worse than traitors for signing the Treaty of New Echota, and the Ridge party resented the Ross party's control of leadership positions, influence, and tribal funds. The Old Settlers, Ridge party, and recently arrived Ross party tried to establish a common unified government in the new lands in Indian Territory. But each group had become accustomed to acting independently, and tensions between the two parties grew over mutual resentment about each other's previous actions. On June 22, 1839, in a series of coordinated attacks, Major Ridge, John Ridge (Major Ridge's son), and Elias Boudinot (one of Major Ridge's nephews) were murdered at scattered sites in the new Cherokee Nation and Arkansas. Major Ridge died as a direct result of a tribal law he helped establish.

One of the few leaders of the Ridge party to escape murder was Major Ridge's nephew Stand Watie, brother of Elias Boudinot. Stand Watie and a few others were scheduled for assassination by the Cherokee conspirators but were warned by their friends in the Ross party and managed to hide and escape death. Although Chief John Ross was never implicated in the murders, one of his sons, Allen Ross, later admitted to being a conspirator. Some one hundred Cherokees are believed to have been involved in the plot to kill the Ridge party's leaders, but no one was ever formally punished by the

Cherokee tribe or the United States government for the crime. A series of revenge killings between members of the Ross and Ridge parties resulted, much like a traditional blood feud.

Following the murder of his uncle, cousin, and brother, Stand Watie became the new leader of the Ridge party. Born on December 12, 1806, in Oothcaloga, in present Cass County, Georgia, Stand Watie was the son of a Cherokee father and a half-Cherokee mother. His father fought in the Red Stick War against the pro-British Creeks. Watie served as a Cherokee Supreme Court clerk and became an attorney. In 1837 he moved to Indian Territory with his family; he married Sarah Bell in 1843 and had two sons and a daughter. Known as a hard worker, Stand Watie was a businessman who owned several farms, some mills, and a general merchandise store in the northeastern corner of the Cherokee Nation. A man of action and a born leader, he wasted few words and was capable of violence. Watie quickly organized companies of armed Cherokees to protect members of the Ridge party against the Ross party. Chief Ross and members of his family then fled to Fort Gibson, where the United States Army protected them from Stand Watie and the Ridge party.

With the Ridge party leadership gone, the new Cherokee Constitution, which had been strongly debated, was quickly approved in the fall of 1839. It provided for executive, legislative, and judicial branches modeled after the United States Constitution. The legislative branch, called the National Council, would draw elected representatives from the eight Cherokee districts. The executive branch consisted of the principal chief, assistant principal chief, and treasurer. The judicial branch contained the Cherokee Supreme Court, various judges, and justices of the peace. The main supporters of this Constitution were the majority Ross party and many Old Settlers.

Between 1839 and 1846 dozens of political murders occurred between the Ridge and Ross parties. In 1843 Stand Watie killed James Foreman, who was rumored to be one of the murderers of Watie's uncle, cousin, and brother, in a fight. After a tense Cherokee trial, Watie was acquitted on grounds of self-defense. In 1845 another of Stand Watie's brothers, Thomas Watie, and Stand Watie's close friend James Starr were murdered.[6]

6. Wardell, *Political History*, 53.

The bloodbath between the Ridge and Ross parties ended with the Treaty of 1846, signed in Washington, D.C., by representatives of the Old Settlers, the Ridge party, and the Ross party. It gave amnesty to fugitives of various crimes if they returned to the Cherokee Nation by December 1, 1846; provided for equal protection of all inhabitants; guaranteed trial by jury; decreed that all lands in the Cherokee Nation were for the use of all Cherokees; and set aside $115,000 for losses suffered by the Ridge party, including $5,000 for each heir of Major Ridge, John Ridge, and Elias Boudinot. Among the signers were Chief John Ross and John Drew.[7]

Homes, schools, churches, and entire communities were built in the new Cherokee Nation by the united Eastern and Western Bands of Cherokees who had emigrated there. The Ross party continued to control the Cherokee government because it outnumbered the Ridge party. Though torn by political warfare in the 1830s and 1840s, the Cherokees made considerable social progress in the 1850s. When the Civil War broke out, Chief John Ross was seventy years old. In spite of his advanced age, he still held tightly to the reins of the Cherokee government.

With the formation of the Confederate States of America and the firing on Fort Sumter in Charleston Harbor in early 1861, the Cherokee Nation was caught between two warring sides. The Nation was bounded on the north by the strong pro-Union state of Kansas, on the northeast by Quapaws and Senecas as well as the divided border state of Missouri, and on the east by the Confederate state of Arkansas. Its southern boundaries were with the pro-Confederate Choctaw Nation and the Creek Nation, and the western boundaries were with the wild Plains Indians. Because of the Union's need for experienced regular army officers and the remoteness of Federal army posts in Indian Territory, the forts there were gradually abandoned. Some officers and soldiers in the United States Army at these posts resigned and rode south or east, joining the Confederate army. The Federal posts at Fort Smith and Little Rock were turned over without a fight to Confederate Arkansas troops and posts in Texas to Confederate Texas troops.

Abandoned by the Federal forces and courted by the Confederate states of Arkansas and Texas, the civilized Indian nations were inclined to sign treaties with the Confederate States after negotiations

7. Woodward, *Cherokees*, 236–37.

with the Confederate commissioner to the Indian nations, Chief Ross's old friend Albert Pike. Pike had been born on December 29, 1809, in Boston, Massachusetts, and attended Harvard College at the age of sixteen but was forced to quit for lack of money. He became a writer, teacher, trader, newspaperman with the Little Rock *Advocate*, and attorney. During the Mexican War, Pike recruited an Arkansas cavalry company and fought as a captain at the Battle of Buena Vista. Pike learned several Indian languages and represented many of the Indian nations on legal matters. He recovered over $2,981,247 for the Choctaws on an old claim against the United States. He was appointed Confederate commissioner to the Indian nations in March, 1861, because of his friendship with the Indians and was commissioned as a brigadier general in the Confederate army on August 15, 1861.[8]

After the formation of the Confederate States, the Plains Indians, as well as the Five Civilized Tribes (Cherokees, Creeks, Seminoles, Chickasaws, and Choctaws), sent delegates to meet at Antelope Hills in the western reaches of Indian Territory to discuss what position to take in the white man's war. Chief John Ross sent Cherokee delegates to the Antelope Hills council to encourage neutrality and to develop plans for all Indians to take advantage of the white man's ills to strengthen Indian sovereignty. Also present with the neutral Cherokees were Creek delegates from the towns that followed Opothleyahola, an old Creek chief who strongly favored the United States. Albert Pike outmaneuvered the Indian council at Antelope Hills by making a treaty with the pro-Confederate leaders in the Creek Nation while those who desired neutrality were at the Antelope Hills council. As neighboring tribes came under the Stars and Bars, the pressure grew on the Cherokees to declare for the South.

Many Cherokees, however, wanted to follow their friends the northern missionaries and remain pro-Union or at least neutral in the impending struggle. The missionaries, who had lived among the Cherokees since before the Trail of Tears, had served as teachers and religious leaders. Chief John Ross's second wife, Mary B. Stapler, was a Quaker from Wilmington, Delaware, whom the chief had married in Philadelphia in 1844, when he was fifty-four and she was eighteen. Chief Ross's wife's family was in the North and he had

8. Wardell, *Political History*, 128; Woodward, *Cherokees*, 259.

no desire to alienate them. Some Cherokees disliked Southerners because the people of Alabama, Georgia, North Carolina, and Tennessee had forced the Federal government to evict the Indians from their ancestral homes and moved them to Indian Territory. Other Cherokees disliked the Texans because several Cherokee and Seminole settlements in Texas had been attacked and destroyed by white Texans with support and aid from the Republic of Texas. Civil war was on the verge of erupting between the Ross and Ridge parties as old hatreds again flared over the question of slavery and the dissolution of the United States. These issues, however, were not the primary reason for division among the Cherokees. The main reason was hatred caused by the Treaty of New Echota and the murders that followed.

Even northern politicians made the Cherokees feel uneasy. William H. Seward, in a speech during the election of 1860, was quoted as saying, "Indian Territory south of Kansas must be vacated by the Indian." Southern secessionists claimed that the abolitionists of the North wanted the Indians' land for greedy white farmers. When Seward became secretary of state, some Indians feared another Trail of Tears.[9]

Stand Watie, Chief Ross's nemesis, was the captain of a company formed to defend members of the minority Ridge party from the larger Ross party. From Arkansas on May 18, 1861, J. Woodward Washbourne and A. M. Wilson wrote to Captain Watie asking the Cherokees "to join in our efforts for mutual defense" and urging Watie to hasten in organizing pro-Confederate Cherokee companies. Washbourne, a former Seminole agent for the United States government, was the son of western Cherokee missionary Cephus Washbourne, was married to one of John and Susan Ridge's daughters, and was thus one of Stand Watie's in-laws. A. M. Wilson was an Arkansas attorney. Washbourne and Wilson promised the pro-Confederate Cherokees arms in six to eight weeks. With the weapons and support from the Confederate state of Arkansas, Watie soon organized a battalion of Cherokees for the Confederacy. On July 12, 1861, he was commissioned a colonel in the Confederate army. Meanwhile, the Ross party and the rest of the Cherokee Nation remained officially neutral. Watie's battalion of about three hundred men was stationed near the Arkansas–Cherokee Nation

9. Woodward, *Cherokees*, 254.

border, scouting into Kansas and Missouri to keep Jayhawkers and Kansas abolitionists out of the Cherokee Nation and Arkansas.[10]

A contingent of Cherokees participated in the important Confederate victory on August 10, 1861, at the Battle of Wilson's Creek or Oak Hills, Missouri, just southwest of Springfield. Joel Mayes, a well-known Cherokee cattleman, was the captain of a Cherokee company serving as scout to Brigadier General Ben McCulloch's Confederate army of Arkansas, Louisiana, Missouri, and Texas troops. Mayes and his men appear to have been part of Watie's battalion. It was reported after the Battle of Wilson's Creek that some Union troops were found scalped on the battlefield and Captain Mayes's Cherokees were prime suspects. The Cherokees returned to their Nation when General McCulloch started enforcing strict military discipline in camp.[11]

The Confederate victories at Bull Run, Virginia, and Wilson's Creek, Missouri, forced the Cherokee Nation to take a hard look at its official position of neutrality. The Cherokees had been abandoned by the Federal government, which had more pressing matters for its attention than a group of Indians west of the Mississippi River. Confederate armies were just a few miles from Washington, D.C., threatening the entire eastern seaboard. All the other Indian nations on the Cherokees' borders as well as the neighboring states of Arkansas and Texas had already joined the Confederate camp. Southern Missouri was pro-Confederate and was occupied by the victorious Confederates. With Colonel Stand Watie leading a battalion of Confederate Cherokees and Chief Ross and his followers lacking any military protection, Ross found it increasingly difficult to maintain neutrality. Ross and many members of his party were sure that Colonel Stand Watie, the prosecessionist Ridge party supporters, and their Confederate allies would cause the Cherokee Nation to join the Confederacy, by "force, if necessary."[12]

Furthermore, the Federal Indian agents had deserted the Cherokee Nation or joined the Confederacy, and the United States had not paid the annuities owed to the Indian nations. In an effort to prevent civil war between Watie's Confederate followers and his

10. J. W. Washbourne and A. M. Wilson to Watie, in Cherokee Nation Papers, Watie Miscellaneous, May 18, 1861, Western History Collection, University of Oklahoma, Norman.

11. Franks, *Stand Watie*, 79–80.

12. Cherokee Resolution of August 21, 1861, in Cherokee Nation Papers.

own followers, Chief John Ross called for all Cherokee citizens to meet at the Cherokee capital of Tahlequah to settle the question of neutrality. The stage was set for the Cherokees to solve by democratic means the questions tearing apart their nation.

2
Formation of the Regiment

On August 21, 1861, the great Cherokee council on the question of neutrality was held in the public square at Tahlequah, a small village just west of the Illinois River at the site of a United States government supply depot at the time of the Cherokee migration. Tahlequah was chosen as the capital of the unified Eastern and Western Bands of the Cherokees because of its central location. The settlement of Park Hill, where Chief Ross and many leaders of the Cherokee Nation lived, was only a few miles southeast of Tahlequah.

About four thousand Cherokee males from all over the Nation attended the important August meeting. Some had to travel for several days to reach Tahlequah. Prominent among those attending the historic council was Colonel Stand Watie and fifty to sixty armed men from his Confederate Cherokee battalion. Watie said he and his companions had come armed to the meeting "to protect themselves from assassination." To some Cherokees, however, such a large force of armed men seemed intimidating, especially since Watie's men vehemently supported abandoning neutrality and making a treaty with the Confederate States of America. The Watie faction's fanatical support of the Confederacy appeared to be a precursor of violence toward their fellow Cherokees.[1]

The majority of the Cherokee citizens who spoke at the meeting favored a treaty with the Confederacy, which offered far more advantageous terms than the old treaties with the United States. The resulting Confederate-Cherokee treaty included a guarantee of Cherokee sovereignty, purchase of the Cherokee Neutral Lands (which the Cherokees had been trying to sell to the United States for years) for $500,000 plus interest, and many financial provisions already in treaties with the United States. The Federal Cherokee agent, Joseph Crawford, had resigned his position in June, 1861, and attended the meeting as a Confederate States agent. There were

1. Grant Foreman Papers, Vol. 39, Box 23, 37, Thomas Gilcrease Institute of American History and Art, Tulsa, Okla.

no United States government representatives present to lobby for Cherokee neutrality or a pro-Union position. The speeches were thus very one-sided in favor of a treaty with the Confederacy. The abolitionist Reverend Evan Jones was reportedly at the meeting, but there is no evidence that he lobbied for the Union.[2]

From the speaker's stand in the Tahlequah public square Chief John Ross addressed the Cherokees in their native language, saying the United States had not asked them to go to war and the Confederacy had observed their neutrality. Alexander (Anthony) Foreman, a Southern secessionist, translated Chief Ross's speech into English for those who could not understand Cherokee. The Confederacy asked the Cherokees to treat with it and to form military units to fight against the Union. The old chief said, "The great object with me has been to have the Cherokee peoples harmonious and united in the full and free exercise and enjoyment of all their rights of person and property. Union is strength; dissension is weakness, misery, ruin." He referred to what would happen should the Indians split apart, as had the United States, and become a divided people. Since most of their brother Indians had already allied themselves with the Confederate States of America, as had the bordering states of Arkansas and Texas, Chief John Ross recommended an alliance with the Confederacy as in the best interests of the Cherokees and Indians in general. Chief John Ross, who wanted only peace and unity among his people, decided to follow the apparent popular sentiment and ally with the Confederacy. Chief Ross felt that the recent Confederate victories ensured the swift defeat of the North in its attempt to reunite the United States of America.[3]

After Chief Ross finished his speech urging the Cherokees "to adopt preliminary steps for an alliance with the Confederate States," Cherokee agent Colonel Joseph Crawford spoke for the Confederacy. Assistant Principal Chief Joseph Vann, a large slaveholder, who favored secession and disliked the secret pro-Union Keetoowah Society, was elected president of the meeting. William Potter Ross, Chief Ross's nephew and heir apparent, was chosen to serve as the meeting's secretary. After a break for dinner, Pickens M. Benge presented a series of resolutions, which were read

2. *The War of the Rebellion: A Compilation of the Official Records of the Union and Confederate Armies* (130 vols.; Washington, D.C., 1880–1901), III, 673, 675 (hereinafter cited as *OR*). Unless otherwise indicated, all citations are to Series I.
3. *Ibid.*, 673–74.

in both English and Cherokee. One resolution declared: "That, reposing full confidence in the constituted authorities of the Cherokee Nation, we submit to their wisdom the management of all questions which affect our interests growing out of the exigencies of the relations between the United and Confederate States of America and which may render an alliance on our part with the latter States expedient and desirable." The motion to accept the alliance with the Confederacy and to repudiate the treaties with the United States was agreed to by acclamation of the Cherokee citizens with no dissenting voices.[4]

Stand Watie's men were ready to lead pro-Confederate Cherokees into declaring the Cherokee Nation a member of the Confederacy and were poised to drive Chief John Ross and his family from control of the Cherokee leadership if Ross did not favor a Confederate-Cherokee treaty. Wily old Chief Ross, however, hoped to prevent a civil war among his people and orchestrated events accordingly. Stand Watie would be allowed no further encroachment into Chief Ross's firm control of the leadership of the Cherokee Nation.[5]

The Cherokee Executive Committee wrote to inform Confederate Brigadier General Ben McCulloch in Arkansas of the Tahlequah council's unanimous decision to join the Confederacy. The Executive Committee, composed of Chief John Ross, James Vann, James Brown, John Drew, and William Potter Ross, also informed General McCulloch of the creation of a Cherokee mounted regiment. In a letter dated August 24, 1861, they wrote: "To be prepared for any such emergency, we have deemed it prudent to proceed to organize a regiment of mounted men and tender them for service. They will be raised forthwith by Col. John Drew, and if received by you will require to be armed. Having abandoned our neutrality and espoused the cause of the Confederate States, we are ready and willing to do all in our powers to advance and sustain it." Thus the Cherokee National Council, a legislative body, agreed to raise John Drew's Regiment of Cherokee Mounted Rifles as the Cherokee government's defense force. Drew's regiment, which favored the Ross party, would also serve as a counterbalance to Watie's battalion of Ridge party supporters.[6]

4. *Ibid.*, 675–76.
5. *Ibid.*, 673–76.
6. *Ibid.*, 673.

Chief Ross sent C. R. Hicks and Joshua Ross to inform Confederate Commissioner Albert Pike of the decision of the Cherokee meeting. Pike was near Fort Arbuckle in the southwest portion of Indian Territory. He received Chief Ross's message on September 3, 1861, and then sent his own messages to the Osages, Shawnees, Quapaws, and Senecas asking them to send their chiefs to meet with him and the Cherokees on September 25 at Park Hill in the Cherokee Nation.[7]

Members of the Ridge party felt frustrated and outflanked because Chief Ross still controlled all government power in the Cherokee Nation in spite of the political intrigues and scheming by the Ridge party. The way Chief Ross raised the question of Cherokee neutrality at the convention in Tahlequah led William Penn Adair of the Ridge party to write, "Ross' Convention . . . tied up our hands & shut our mouths" and the "Pins [Keetoowahs] already have more power in this land than we can bear." Members of the Ridge party felt that the old chief was trying to maneuver them into a position of submission, denying them any political power even though they had been the ones who originally favored supporting the Confederacy. Upon hearing of Chief Ross's plan to raise a regiment under Colonel Drew, James M. Bell, Stand Watie's brother-in-law, immediately wrote to Colonel Watie: "It will require a rapid . . . movement on our part or else we are all done up. All of our work will be in vain. Our prospects destroyed our rights disregarded and we will be *slaves* to Ross' Tyranny." Bell wanted Watie to counter the Ross party's move to raise its own regiment. Undoubtedly, Watie approached his friends in the Confederacy with the notion of expanding his battalion into a regiment under his command so that the Ridge party would be on an equal military footing with the Ross party.[8]

On September 1, 1861, Brigadier General Ben McCulloch replied to Colonel John Drew from his headquarters at Fayetteville, Arkansas: "As soon as a treaty Can be entered into between your Chiefs and General Pike your regiment will be received and mustered into service." General McCulloch noted in separate letters to both Chief Ross and newly appointed Colonel John Drew that the Confederacy

7. Charles Lee Bahos, "John Ross: Unionist or Secessionist in 1861?" (Master's thesis, University of Tulsa, 1968), 83–84.

8. W. P. Adair and James M. Bell to Watie, August 29, 1861, in Cherokee Nation Papers, Watie Miscellaneous.

had also just authorized Colonel Stand Watie to raise a regiment to assist in the protection of the northern boundary of the Cherokee Nation from a possible Union invasion. So as not to disturb the Cherokee neutrality until a formal Confederate-Cherokee treaty was signed, General McCulloch kept all of his Confederate Indian units outside the boundaries of the Cherokee Nation. Thus Colonel Stand Watie's followers and Chief Ross's followers were segregated into rival Confederate units with different political loyalties. Watie's battalion was expanded into a regiment no doubt to counter Chief Ross's raising of a regiment of Ross party supporters.[9]

On September 2, 1861, General McCulloch wrote Leroy Pope Walker, the Confederate secretary of war, strongly suggesting that Watie's battalion of mixed-bloods be maintained as a separate unit from the full-bloods in Drew's regiment. McCulloch believed that the recent Confederate victory at Wilson's Creek (or Oak Hills as the Confederates called it) had caused Chief John Ross finally to abandon neutrality and join the Confederate States. McCulloch wrote, "Colonel Drew's Regiment will be mostly composed of full-bloods, whilst those with Col. Stand Watie will be half-breeds, who are educated men, and good soldiers anywhere, in or out of the Nation." Soon afterward Watie's battalion was officially expanded into a regiment.[10]

Both Watie's and Drew's regiments claimed the right to be called the 1st Regiment of Cherokee Mounted Rifles. Both appear in official correspondence as either the 1st or 2d Regiment of Cherokees or Cherokee Mounted Rifles, depending on the politics of the person who wrote the letter as well as to whom the letter was addressed. To halt further confusion and arguments over regimental names, each Cherokee regiment was finally referenced by the name of its commander.

The staff selected by Chief Ross to lead Colonel Drew's newly formed regiment was composed of loyal members of the Ross party, many of whom were close relatives of Chief John Ross. Almost all of the officers held or had held various political positions within the Cherokee government. To a large extent the officers were treated as political appointees chosen by Chief Ross, rather than as leaders elected by their men as was done in other Confederate regiments.

9. *OR*, III, 690–92.
10. *Ibid.*, 692.

Chief Ross wanted to be sure that Drew's regiment would be loyal to him and respond to his commands.

John Drew, selected as colonel and commander of the Ross party's regiment of Cherokees, was Chief John Ross's nephew-in-law, married to Chief Ross's niece Maria Coody. John Drew was a prominent Cherokee citizen who lived at Webbers Falls on the Arkansas River. As the owner of several salt works and a few slaves, he was considered a rich man in the Cherokee Nation. His sentiments were generally those of a secessionist. John Drew signed the Cherokee Constitution at Tahlequah on September 6, 1839, and had served as the Canadian District's senator. Like Chief John Ross, he fought on the side of the United States against the pro-British Creeks during the War of 1812. Drew's title before the Civil War was captain, probably from his organization of a Cherokee company of mounted men in 1842. That company had rounded up escaped Cherokee-owned Negro slaves who had fled from Webbers Falls to find freedom in the wilds of the Spanish territory to the west. Some of these fugitive slaves belonged to John Drew's neighbor "Rich Joe" Vann. Drew's company of about a hundred men chased the band of some two hundred escaped slaves into what is now western Oklahoma, captured them, and returned them to the Cherokee Nation with few problems.[11] In a letter dated January 10, 1860, John Vann suggested that Captain John Drew become the leader of a local secessionist company, which would patrol the Canadian District in search of escaped slaves, guard against abolitionists, and compel "all negroes to know their places."[12]

In July, 1861, a company of pro-Southern Cherokees attempted to raise the Confederate flag over Webbers Falls. William Doublehead, a Canadian District senator, and 150 full-bloods confronted the Confederate Cherokee supporters and a fight appeared imminent. William Doublehead reportedly had been involved in the conspiracy that resulted in the murder of Major Ridge in 1839, so bad blood existed between him and the Ridge party.[13]

Many of the Confederate supporters present at the confrontation at Webbers Falls were members of the Ridge party. John Drew

11. Wardell, *Political History*, 119.
12. Carolyn Thomas Foreman, "Early History of Webbers Falls," *Chronicles of Oklahoma*, XXIX (Winter, 1951–52), 469.
13. T. L. Ballenger, "The Death and Burial of Major Ridge," *Chronicles of Oklahoma*, LI (Spring, 1973), 102.

played a major part in preventing bloodshed between the two groups, and he cooled the hot tempers of their leaders. Drew was respected for his actions by both the Ross and Ridge parties and thus appeared to be a good choice for commander of the new Cherokee regiment.[14] At the date of the mustering in of Drew's regiment on November 5, 1861, the rolls showed Colonel Drew to be sixty-five years of age. His rather advanced age would later limit his ability to campaign actively and to control the much younger members of the regiment.

William Potter Ross, Chief John Ross's nephew, was selected as lieutenant colonel of Drew's regiment. He was an unwavering supporter of Chief Ross and continued to be the protégé of the old chief. It appears that Chief Ross was grooming his nephew to become the leader of the Ross party and principal chief of the Cherokee Nation. William P. Ross's education was paid for by Chief John Ross when financial problems prevented his father from sending him to school. In 1842 William P. Ross graduated with honors, first in a class of forty-four, from Princeton College. He served as Cherokee Senate clerk in 1843; was editor of the Cherokee-language newspaper, the *Cherokee Advocate*, from 1844 to 1848, and married his first cousin Mary Jane (Mollie) Ross, Lewis Ross's daughter, in 1846. Lewis Ross was the brother of Chief John Ross and of William P. Ross's mother. Starting in 1860, William P. Ross served as secretary to the Cherokee national secretary, Lewis Ross, who also was his father-in-law and uncle. William P. Ross was an attorney and merchant in Fort Gibson and was also involved in the Ross family businesses. At the date of his mustering into Drew's regiment, he was forty-one years old.[15]

The major of Drew's regiment was Thomas Pegg, a noted politician who had served as a Cherokee representative lobbying the U.S. government in Washington, D.C., in 1859. Pegg was also president of the Cherokee National Committee and served as a senator from the Saline District from 1853 to 1855. At the date he was mustered into the regiment, Major Pegg was fifty-three.[16]

---

14. J. P. Evans to Chief Ross, July 2, 1861, in John Ross Papers, 61-24 (the first numeral refers to the year, the second to the item or paper), Thomas Gilcrease Institute of American History and Art, Tulsa, Okla., and Chief Ross to Drew, July 2, 1861, *ibid.*, 61-25.
15. Mrs. William P. Ross (ed.), *The Life and Times of Hon. William P. Ross* (Ft. Smith, Ark., 1893), n.p.
16. Wardell, *Political History,* 171.

Chosen as adjutant of Drew's regiment was James Springston Vann, the son of Colonel Drew's longtime neighbor "Rich Joe" Vann and also Lieutenant Colonel William P. Ross's brother-in-law through his marriage to Aramita Ross, Mary Jane Ross's sister. Vann inherited much wealth from his father's estate, traveled to California during the Gold Rush in 1849, and in 1861 was a resident of Webbers Falls. He was known to have pro-Union sympathies. The regimental roster shows James S. Vann to be thirty-nine years old at the date of mustering.[17]

The expressman of Drew's regiment was Frederick Augustus Kerr, the husband of John Ross's niece Louisa Jan Coody.[18] Israel G. Vore was selected as regimental quartermaster because of his skill at merchandising. Vore was married to Adjutant James S. Vann's sister Sarah, also called Sally. Vore's parents had been traders and were murdered at their trading post in 1843. He was a traveling Baptist preacher and was actively engaged in raising cattle and operating three trading posts. At the date of mustering, Quartermaster Vore was forty years old.[19]

Frederick Augustus Kerr appears to have taken over most of the quartermaster duties shortly after the formation of the regiment. Obtaining supplies in the Cherokee Nation was no easy feat because of the uncertainties of transportation. But Kerr was talented at organizing and transporting supplies. At the time of mustering he was forty-nine years old.[20]

The regiment's chaplain was the Reverend Lewis Downing, who had attended the Baptist Mission under the Reverend Evan Jones and was an ordained Baptist minister. His grandfather was a major in the British army. The Reverend Downing served both as a Cherokee senator and an official Cherokee representative to Washington, D.C. Downing was thirty-eight at the time of mustering.[21]

On October 5, 1861, Colonel Drew appointed his friend Dr. James P. Evans surgeon of the regiment. Evans' son Walter N. Evans aided

17. Grant Foreman, *Marcy and the Gold Seekers* (Norman, 1968), 68.

18. Hanna Hicks, "The Diary of Hanna Hicks," *American Scene*, XIII, No. 3 (1972), 23.

19. Carolyn Thomas Foreman, "Israel G. Vore and Levering Manual Labor School," *Chronicles of Oklahoma*, XXV (Autumn, 1947), 198–201.

20. Marguerite McFadden, "The Saga of 'Rich Joe' Vann," *Chronicles of Oklahoma*, LXI (Spring, 1983), 77–78.

21. John Bartlett Meserve, "Chief Lewis Downing and Chief Charles Thompson (Oochalata)," *Chronicles of Oklahoma*, XVI (September, 1938), 317–18.

him as the regiment's hospital steward. Dr. Joseph W. Carden served as the regiment's assistant surgeon.[22] Two of Chief John Ross's sons also enlisted in Drew's regiment. Sergeant Allen Ross and Second Lieutenant George Washington Ross were both in Company H.

With so many political and family appointments, the officers of Drew's regiment included the cream of the Cherokee aristocracy: politicians, businessmen, ranchers, and lawyers—all close associates of the Ross party. Many officers were directly related to Chief Ross and were mixed-blood Cherokees.

22. J. P. Evans to Chief Ross, July 2, 1861, in John Drew Papers, 61-24, Gilcrease Institute of American History and Art, Tulsa, Oklahoma.

3
Organization and the Creek Problem

When it was recruited, John Drew's Regiment of Cherokee Mounted Rifles stood to benefit from several favorable clauses in the proposed Confederate treaty with the Cherokee Nation. The treaty stated that the government of the Confederate States of America would arm the Cherokees; the Cherokees would receive the same pay allowances as regular Confederate soldiers; and the Indians would not be required to leave the Indian nations for military ventures "without their consent." The members of each company in the Indian unit were to select their own officers, with the field officers being selected by the regiment, but Confederate President Jefferson Davis was to appoint the regiment's colonel, as was common in the Confederate army.[1]

These incentives helped to recruit Cherokees to fill the eleven companies of Drew's regiment. McDaniel's company was formed as a reserve company, and a second reserve company was created but not filled. Each company was recruited in a separate Cherokee district, with the exception of the Tahlequah District, in which Companies B, H, and I were recruited. Company A was from the Saline District, Company C from the Canadian District, Company D from the Delaware District, Company E from the Flint District, Company F from the Illinois District, Company G from the Going Snake District, Company K from the Sequoyah District, and McDaniel's Reserve Company from the Cooweescoowee District.

As a rule, in Drew's regiment the enlisted men were full-bloods and the officers were mixed-bloods and affiliated with the Ross party. A good percentage of these officers were directly related to Chief John Ross and his immediate family. A list of officers by company in Drew's regiment on November 5, 1861, is presented as Appendix I. A copy of the muster roll of Drew's Regiment of Cherokee Mounted Rifles on November 5, 1861, is shown as Appendix II.

1. *OR*, Ser. IV, Vol. I, 679.

The officers tended to be educated men and had English names, but the full-blood Cherokees generally went by their Indian names. Most Cherokees had English Christian names as well as Cherokee names. Often their Cherokee names were translated into English, resulting in one person being called by as many as three different sets of names. Spellings of each name varied widely depending on each person's ability to read and write. This system, of course, has resulted in much confusion in written records and makes it difficult to follow records relating to service, especially among the full-bloods.

Most of the enlisted men in the regiment were members of the Keetoowah Society, a secret organization of full-bloods founded by two abolitionist Baptist preachers, the Reverend Evan Jones and his son the Reverend John Buttrick Jones. The Reverend Evan Jones was born in Wales in 1788, where he was a member of the Church of England. He became a Methodist and converted to a Baptist upon emigrating to the United States. In 1821, the Reverend Evan Jones became a Baptist missionary to Cherokees in North Carolina and migrated to Indian Territory with the Cherokees in 1838. His son John Buttrick Jones was born in North Carolina in 1824, graduated from the University of Rochester, became a Baptist minister in 1855, and served with his father at the Baptist Mission a few miles south-west of present Westville, Oklahoma.[2] The Keetoowah Society was organized in 1859 to preserve the religious and moral code of the old Keetoowah Society, which had been abandoned some years before. Its members were Christians who wanted to preserve ancient Cherokee tribal rites. It started among a Baptist congregation at Peavine in the Cherokee Nation's Going Snake District and soon spread throughout the Nation. The Loyal League was formed in late 1860 or early 1861 and contained mostly Keetoowahs whose aims were to maintain friendly relations with the United States, to enforce prior Cherokee treaties, and to keep from political office and power every man suspected of treason against the Cherokee Nation and the United States. Some two thousand Cherokees were reported to have belonged to the secret Loyal League, all of them Chief John Ross's followers. Some three thousand Cherokees were reported to have belonged to the Keetoowah Society. Both groups were formed in part to oppose the Blue Lodge and the Knights of the Golden

2. Meserve, "Downing and Thompson," 315–16.

Circle, which were secret prosecession organizations made up of mixed-blood Indians and white men.[3]

The Baptist Mission Board recalled the Reverends Evan Jones and John B. Jones from their congregations in the Cherokee Nation in mid-1861 because of the controversy they stirred up between the proslavery and antislavery factions of the Nation.[4] In September, 1861, the Reverend John B. Jones was ordered by the pro-Confederate Cherokee agent to leave the Cherokee Nation within three weeks because of an article in a northern newspaper that quoted him as saying he was strongly promoting antislavery sentiments among his Cherokee Indian congregation.[5]

The main goals of the Keetoowah Society and the Loyal League seem to have been abolishing slavery and preventing the mixed-bloods of the Ridge party from taking control of the Cherokee government. As an indication of their loyalty to the United States government the Keetoowahs chose the United States flag and crossed pins as their society's emblem. These pins were worn on the coat, vest, or shirt. From this emblem they earned the nickname "pins." Correspondence in 1861 generally used that term to refer to the Keetoowahs, but later it came to mean Union Indians in general. Members of the Keetoowah Society met in secret on mountains, in forests, and in caves to pledge allegiance to the United States and to plot against members of the Ridge party.[6]

Keetoowah membership was reserved for full-blood Cherokees who were uneducated and had no mixed-blood friends. This organization excluded most officers in Drew's regiment. The Keetoowahs were also a fraternal organization. Death was the punishment for anyone revealing the secret society's activities.[7] The Keetoowahs had secret signs with which to identify one another. From a distance they could touch their hats in a salute. They also had a special way of holding the lapel of their coats, drawing it away from their bodies and giving a motion as though wrapping it around their hearts.[8]

3. Mooney, "Myths of the Cherokee," 225–26.

4. Wardell, *Political History,* 120–23.

5. Charles C. Royce, "The Cherokee Nation of Indians," in *Fifth Annual Report of the Bureau of Ethnology to the Secretary at the Smithsonian Institution* (Washington, D.C., 1887), 202–203.

6. Howard Q. Tyner, "The Keetoowach Society in Cherokee History" (Master's thesis, University of Tulsa, 1949), 25, 31–34.

7. *Ibid.,* 104–106.

8. Mooney, "Myths of the Cherokee," 226.

To initiate the recruiting of Drew's regiment, the Confederate army on September 2, 1861, authorized Colonel John Drew to buy "a sufficient quantity of fresh beef and salt; to ration the members" of his regiment as they came into camp to be organized. George W. Clarke, the Confederate quartermaster at Fort Smith, wrote Colonel Drew on September 19 that he would soon send him copies of muster rolls. When Drew was granted final authority by the Confederate government, he was to muster his men into the regiment. Officially Drew's regiment was not mustered into the service of the Confederacy but was in the service of the Cherokee Nation.[9]

In the Creek Nation a loyal faction declared the Confederate treaty with the Creeks illegal and selected Oktarharsars Harjo or Sands to act as their principal chief. The Creeks, like the Cherokees, were divided politically into two parties. The Loyal or pro-Union Creeks gathered around Opothleyahola, an old Upper Creek chief who was born about 1798 in the old Creek Nation. Opothleyahola was known variously as Opothleyaholo, Hopoeithleyohola, Hopoth leyahola, and Opothle Yahola. He is believed to have fought with the Red Stick Creeks against the United States in the War of 1812. As a speaker in the Upper Creek Council in the old tradition, Opothleyahola fought hard against removal of the Indians from the Southeast but was forced to move to Indian Territory in 1836. At the start of the Civil War, Opothleyahola controlled about two thousand acres of land near North Fork Town which many Negro slaves farmed for him. Although a great leader, Opothleyahola could neither read nor write. He resisted the efforts of pro-Confederate Creeks, led by half-brothers Daniel N. ("Dode") McIntosh and Chilly McIntosh, who were also leaders of the Lower Creeks, against the United States.[10]

Daniel N. McIntosh and Chilly McIntosh were the sons of a Creek chief, General William McIntosh, who was murdered in 1828 in Georgia by Opothleyahola's followers for signing the Treaty of Indian Springs. This treaty ceded all Creek lands in Georgia and a portion of Creek lands in Alabama to the United States in exchange for new lands in Indian Territory. Civil war between the two rival Creek parties had been only narrowly averted before the start of the Civil War through the efforts of each party's leaders.

9. Clarke to Drew, September 2, 19, 1861, in Drew Papers, 61-14, 61-18.
10. John Bartlett Meserve, "Chief Opothleyahola," *Chronicles of Oklahoma*, IX (December, 1931), 445–53.

The Upper Creeks originally lived in towns on the upper tributaries of the Chattahoochee River in Alabama and Georgia, while the Lower Creeks lived in towns on the lower reaches of the river. Upper Creeks tended to honor their treaties with the United States. The Loyal Creeks along with a few pro–United States members of other Indian tribes gathered together and called on the Federal Indian agents in Kansas for immediate aid from the United States government. The Loyal Creeks feared their political antagonists would strike against them at any time. Colonel Daniel N. McIntosh and Lieutenant Colonel Chilly McIntosh were the leaders of the newly formed Confederate 1st Creek Regiment, composed of Lower Creeks. Colonel Daniel McIntosh, like many leaders of the time, was also an ordained Baptist minister. Both McIntosh brothers hoped to avenge old wrongs against their family caused by Opothleyahola and his followers. Their situation was very similar to that facing the Cherokees.[11]

Although there was as yet only a handful of men in Drew's regiment, Colonel Daniel McIntosh, as commander of the newly formed Confederate 1st Creek Regiment, asked Colonel Drew and his Cherokee Mounted Rifles to hasten to the Creek Nation to help quell the rising dissent of the band of pro-Union Creeks led by Opothleyahola. McIntosh was alarmed by the growing number of Creeks who refused to pledge allegiance to the Confederacy and wrote Colonel Drew that the Cherokee Nation also faced danger; it was not just a Creek problem. In answer to McIntosh's requests, the newly formed 1st Choctaw and Chickasaw Regiment came to his aid.[12]

Negroes in the Indian Nations were also joining Opothleyahola's band of dissidents, and the Confederates feared that the free Negroes had a powerful influence on some of the Creeks and Seminoles. These Negroes were instrumental in stirring opposition to the Creek treaty with the Confederate States negotiated by Confederate Indian Commissioner Albert Pike. The Creek Nation's General Council passed a law on March 1, 1861, giving free Negroes within the boundaries of the Creek Nation only ten days to choose a master or face sale to the highest Creek bidder. This act coupled with abolitionist preachings caused a great number of Negroes to join

11. Angie Debo, *The Road to Disappearance: A History of the Creek Indians* (Norman, 1979), 147–50.
12. McIntosh to Drew, September 11, 1861, in Drew Papers, 61-17.

Opothleyahola in hope of escaping slavery by finding safety in numbers. The prospect of a slave revolt and of loyal Indians trying to overthrow Confederate Indians on the border of the Cherokee Nation deeply worried the government of Chief John Ross.[13]

Also joining the scattered temporary pro-Union camps of Indians near Opothleyahola's home were forty families of Chickasaws, about one-half of the Seminole tribe, and some Choctaws, Shawnees, Delawares, Comanches, and Kickapoos. Colonel Drew tried to ignore the Creek problem as he gathered his men in the new Cherokee regiment at strategic Fort Gibson, where he would train and organize them.[14]

Fort Gibson was a former United States Army post on the Grand River established in 1824 to guard the Three Forks area, where the Verdigris River and Grand River or Neosho River feed into the Arkansas River. Fort Gibson was the upper end of steamboat navigation of the Arkansas and Grand rivers, and a strategic Indian trail that became the Texas Road passed across the Grand River from Fort Gibson. The Texas Road was sometimes called the Fort Scott–Fort Gibson Military Road because it was a vital link between United States Army frontier forts in Kansas and Indian Territory. The Texas Road was the logical route for any Union army wishing to invade Texas from Kansas so the Confederacy valued control of the Three Forks area.

Fort Gibson and its large United States military reservation had been turned over to the Cherokee Nation in 1857 when the need to protect the Five Civilized Tribes from the hostile Indian tribes to the west and from each other ended. The old fort was an ideal gathering point for Drew's regiment because of its good boat landing, its central location in the Cherokee Nation, and its substantial military barracks and storehouses. Much of the fort and military reservation had been sold to individual Cherokee citizens by the Cherokee Nation, and some called the town around the fort Keetoowah. Lieutenant Colonel William P. Ross's home was also located at Fort Gibson.[15]

To complete their organization, members of the regiment gathered at Fort Gibson on September 23, 1861. They expected to

13. Andre Paul DuChateau, "The Creek Nation on the Eve of the Civil War," *Chronicles of Oklahoma*, LII (Fall, 1974), 299–300.
14. *OR*, Ser. IV, Vol. II, 353–54.
15. Grant Foreman, *Fort Gibson: A Brief History* (Muskogee, Okla., n.d.), 23.

escort Brigadier General Albert Pike to Park Hill, the home of Chief John Ross, the next day to sign the Confederate-Cherokee treaty. As the Confederate commissioner to the Indians west of Arkansas and south of Kansas, Pike did a magnificent job in bringing the Five Civilized Tribes into the Confederate camp.[16]

When Pike arrived at Fort Gibson about October 1, 1861, he was met by eight or nine companies of Colonel John Drew's Regiment of Cherokee Mounted Rifles and escorted to Park Hill. Drew's regiment of some nine hundred men set up camp with General Pike within sight of Chief John Ross's home, Rose Cottage. Rose Cottage was a fine two-story house in the Southern tradition, with a pillared portico and rooms to accommodate forty guests. Leading up to Rose Cottage was a half-mile roadway lined with roses. Chief John Ross had some one hundred slaves, and he had spent $10,000 importing furniture from the East for his home. Numerous outbuildings and slave quarters were located around Rose Cottage. Some thousand apple trees stood in Chief Ross's orchard. After setting up his camp, General Pike ran up a Confederate flag with a red star for each Indian treaty he had successfully completed. This flag was to be a morale booster before starting his negotiations with the Cherokees for a pro-Confederate treaty.[17]

In nearby Tahlequah, companies of Watie's regiment along with Watie's brother-in-law and friend James M. Bell came into town in preparation for the treaty negotiations. As usual, hot feelings existed between the Ross and Ridge factions, and members of the rival groups exchanged inflammatory tracts and words, adding to the hostile atmosphere. Letters to Chief Ross from United States Indian agent E. H. Carruth were widely circulated among the Cherokees by Ridge party supporters without Chief Ross's authorization.[18]

With much ceremony, Pike negotiated with Chief John Ross on October 2 and 4. On October 2 Pike concluded treaty negotiations with the Osages, and on October 4 he signed treaties with representatives of the Quapaws, Senecas, and Shawnees. The treaty negotiations took place in log council houses on the Tahlequah Square in the center of the Cherokee capital of Tahlequah.[19]

16. Drew to Clarke, September 21, 1861, in Drew Papers, 61-19.
17. Robert Lipscomb Duncan, *Reluctant General: The Life and Times of Albert Pike* (New York, 1961), 172–73.
18. John W. Stapler to Chief Ross, September 25, 1861, in Ross Papers, 61-38, Gilcrease Institute.
19. Duncan, *Reluctant General*, 181.

During this time Drew's Regiment of Cherokee Mounted Rifles was officially enrolled for Confederate service. Finally, on October 7, 1861, treaty negotiations were completed and the officers of the regiment were officially commissioned into Confederate service by Brigadier General Albert Pike. In a formal ceremony, Pike presented Colonel Drew's Cherokee regiment with a flag. After the ceremony, Stand Watie, who had eighty or ninety of his men with him, shook hands with his old enemy Chief John Ross and "expressed his warm desire for union and harmony in the Nation."[20]

On October 7, 1861, Pike offered a pardon to Opothleyahola and any other Indians who had followed him in arms against the Confederacy if they would lay down their weapons and join the Confederacy. The one exception was a half-Delaware, half-Negro named Jim Ned, who had signed a treaty with the Confederacy in August, 1861, and broke it by joining the loyal Indians. Pike wanted Opothleyahola's followers to form a battalion of soldiers to serve in the Confederate army.[21]

The next day councils were held with delegations of Osages, Quapaws, Shawnees, and Senecas, who had gathered as requested to negotiate with the Confederate Indian commissioner. These representatives signed treaties of allegiance to the Confederate States of America, but not all members of the tribes signing the treaties were loyal to the Confederacy, especially among the Osages.

On October 8, 1861, Chief John Ross wrote Opothleyahola explaining the reasons for the Cherokees' abandonment of neutrality and asking him to come to Park Hill to meet with General Albert Pike in an effort to come to a mutual understanding to prevent bloodshed among the Indians. The Cherokees had agreed on a Confederate treaty and were in the process of ratifying it while Chief John Ross was communicating with Opothleyahola. General Pike granted a letter of safeguard to Opothleyahola to attend the meeting at Tahlequah. Assistant Cherokee Principal Chief Joseph Vann carried the message personally to Opothleyahola, but the old Creek chief refused to parlay with anyone allied with the Confederacy. Chief Opothleyahola felt betrayed by Chief Ross's abandonment of Cherokee neutrality and his declaration for the Confederacy.[22]

20. *Ibid.*

21. Pike to Opothleyahola, October 7, 1861, in Cherokee Nation Papers.

22. Wardell, *Political History*, 133; Chief Ross to Opothleyahola *et al.*, October 8, 1861, in Ross Papers, 61-41, Gilcrease Institute.

Chief Ross later wrote that his last messenger to Opothleyahola had approval from both Colonel Douglas Hancock Cooper of the 1st Choctaw and Chickasaw Regiment and Colonel Daniel N. McIntosh of the 1st Creek Regiment. Some Loyal Creek chiefs, however, "who were already stripped and painted for war," prevented the messenger from seeing Opothleyahola. Conflict between Opothleyahola's followers and the Confederacy appeared inevitable.[23]

Chief John Ross addressed the Cherokee National Council on October 9, 1861, stressing the need to ratify the Confederate treaty with the Cherokee Nation: "To meet any emergency that might spring upon our Northern border, it was thought proper to raise a Regiment of mounted men and tender its services to General Mc-Culloch. . . . It is now in the service of the Confederate States for the purpose of aiding in defending the homes and the common rights of the Indian Nations about us. This Regiment is composed of 10 full companies with two reserve companies and in addition to the force previously authorized to be raised to operate outside of the Nation by General McCulloch." He emphasized that Drew's regiment was only for the defense of the Cherokee Nation and was not to be sent to the Confederate armies operating in the East. Ross added, "The Cherokee Nation may be called upon to furnish Troops for the defense of the Indian Country but is never to be taxed for the support of any war in which the States may be engaged." The treaty between the Confederate States of America and the Cherokee Nation was quickly ratified by the Cherokee National Council.[24]

During the week-long council at Park Hill, Motley Kennard, a Creek chief at Confederate Camp Pleasant, wrote to Chief John Ross asking the Cherokees to mediate with Opothleyahola and his pro-Union followers. At the same time Colonel Daniel McIntosh appealed to General Albert Pike for more troops to block a feared attack upon his forces by the loyal Indians.[25]

These and numerous other Confederate Creek appeals led Brigadier General Ben McCulloch, the Confederate commander in Arkansas, to order Drew's regiment to "proceed without delay" and

23. Dean Trickett, "The Civil War in the Indian Territory, 1861," *Chronicles of Oklahoma*, XVIII (September, 1940), 268.

24. Chief Ross's Address to the National Cherokee Council, October 9, 1861, in Ross Papers, 61-43, Gilcrease Institute.

25. Motley Kennard to Chief Ross, October 3, 1861, Chief Ross to [?], October 4, 1861, in Ross Papers, 61-40 and 61-41, Gilcrease Institute; Colonel Daniel McIntosh to Pike, October 3, 1861, in Drew Papers, 61-22.

join forces with Colonel Daniel McIntosh's and Colonel Douglas H. Cooper's commands to move against the disaffected Creeks when the Cherokee regiment was fully organized.[26] McCulloch was the son of Brigadier General Alexander McCulloch, who fought with General Andrew Jackson in the War of 1812. Ben McCulloch had a colorful career, serving as commander of Sam Houston's artillery at the Battle of San Jacinto, fighting Indians on the Texas frontier, commanding Texas Rangers in the Mexican War, serving as a United States marshal in California, and accepting the surrender of the United States installations in Texas to the Confederacy in 1861.

To Chief John Ross and many Cherokees, however, the thought of a clash with their Indian brothers and neighbors, the Creeks, whether loyal or disloyal, brought forth bitter resentment. Many Cherokees and Creeks were related by marriage. A number of Indian leaders feared that bloody feuds would continue between the old political factions within the Cherokee and Creek nations once the Civil War was over, regardless of the war's outcome. Worse from the Confederate viewpoint was a newspaper report that Opothleyahola was a "warm friend" of Cherokee Chief John Ross and the true feelings of Chief Ross and his followers might prevent them from acting against the loyal Indians.[27]

Chief John Ross sent a letter to Opothleyahola and others concerning the Cherokee decision, saying, "I am gratified to inform you that the Great Being who over-rules all things for good, has sustained me in my efforts to unite the hearts and sentiments of the Cherokee People as one man," and "with one voice we have proclaimed in favor of forming an alliance with the Confederate States, and shall thereby preserve and maintain the Brotherhood of the Indian Nations in a Common Destiny." Chief John Ross again tried hard to convince Opothleyahola that he really had abandoned neutrality for an alliance with the Confederacy. He wrote to a disbelieving Opothleyahola, "My advice and desire under the present extraordinary crisis, is, for all the red Brethren to be united among themselves in the Support of our common rights—and interest by forming an alliance of Peace and friendship with the Confederate States of America." Chief Ross was promoting Indian unity in the midst of a civil war that divided the whites.[28]

26. McCulloch to Drew, October 6, 1861, in Drew Papers, 61-23.
27. Clarksville *Standard* (Texas), October 26, 1861.
28. Chief Ross to Opothleyahola, September 19, 1861, in Cherokee Nation Papers.

The Confederate Creeks continually pleaded for more troops to forestall the feared attack by Opothleyahola's army. Since the Cherokees were unwilling to aid the Confederate Creeks against the Loyal Creeks, a letter from Confederate army headquarters in Arkansas ordered Colonel Drew, who was at Tahlequah, to march his regiment "to the southern line of Kansas and take position on the Neosho River." At the same time, Colonel Douglas H. Cooper was given overall command of the Confederate Cherokee regiment's movements.[29]

Cooper was the former Choctaw and Chickasaw agent for the United States government and had served in the Indian nations for eight years. During that time he had become known to and respected by all of the Indian tribes. During the Mexican War he was a captain in Jefferson Davis' Mississippi regiment, and he remained a friend of Davis when he became president of the Confederacy. He was a firm proslavery advocate and commanded the first Indian regiment put into Confederate service, the 1st Choctaw and Chickasaw Regiment. Colonel Cooper was the only commander of a Confederate Indian unit from the Indian nations who was not an Indian.

General Albert Pike left Indian Territory for the Confederate capital of Richmond, Virginia, where he hoped to get funds to pay the Indians the sums due them under their treaties. Upon Pike's departure Colonel Cooper became the Confederate commander of Indian Territory. Chief John Ross still believed the divided Creeks could be peacefully reconciled. As conditions deteriorated in the Creek Nation, Chief Ross received a note from a Confederate Creek chief who said there was "no hope for a friendly adjustment of the difficulty." The thought of fellow tribesmen at war with one another appalled the old Cherokee leader who was a prominent advocate of Indian unity.[30]

With this bad news in mind, Chief John Ross, on October 21, 1861, told Colonel John Drew that the affairs of the Cherokee Nation required Drew's attention in his "own Country," thereby trying to prevent a confrontation between the Cherokees and Creeks.[31] Part

29. Armstrong to Drew, October 13, 1861, in Drew Papers, 61-27.

30. Chief Ross and Joseph Vann to Motley Kennard and Echo Harjo, October 20, 1861, and Drew to W. P. Ross, October 20, 1861, in Ross Papers, 61-48 and 61-47, Gilcrease Institute.

31. Chekote to Drew, October 21, 1861, and Cooper to Motley Kennard, October 21, 1861, in Drew Papers, 61-30 and 61-28.

of Drew's regiment then arrived at Camp Porter in the Creek Nation, where Drew was to meet with Cooper to discuss the Creek situation. Cooper gathered together the Confederate Indian Brigade, which consisted of the 1st Choctaw and Chickasaw Regiment, the 1st Creek Regiment, and the Seminole Battalion, to settle the issue of loyalty with the followers of Opothleyahola, by force if necessary. Cooper made plans to hold a council with a delegation from Opothleyahola's camp. This last effort at reconciliation failed because delegates from Opothleyahola's camp could not even agree with the Confederates on how and where to set up a meeting as neither side trusted the other.

In spite of the desires and orders of Chief Ross, Colonel Drew met with Colonel Cooper on October 22 at Camp Porter while the rest of Drew's regiment camped nearby.[32] From this conference Cooper authorized Drew to "purchase . . . such arms as can be procured, at a reasonable price" to complete the arming of his regiment so it could be ready for action. A number of Drew's men were still without suitable weapons. Members of the regiment were to be paid by the Confederate government for any personal arms they used during regimental service. Because of the Creek problem Cooper expected Drew's regiment would need those weapons soon.[33]

After this council Drew's regiment returned to camp at Fort Gibson, leaving Colonel Cooper and his Indian Brigade to face Opothleyahola's followers. Brigadier General Albert Pike later reported to Judah P. Benjamin, the Confederate secretary of war, that the adjutant of Drew's regiment, James S. Vann, had told him of his reluctance to fight against Opothleyahola's Creeks. Pike thought a great many other Cherokees felt the same way, and he was very reluctant to employ Indians against Indians in any fight. The arrival in Indian Territory of newly recruited Texas cavalry regiments allowed Drew's regiment to stay in the Cherokee Nation and thus prevented the Creek issue from being pressed upon them immediately.[34]

Colonel Cooper was determined to disperse Opothleyahola's band and to capture all the Negroes accompanying them, especially the fugitive slaves. Confederate authorities in the slaveholding

32. Cooper to Motley Kennard, October 21, 1861, *ibid.*, 61-30; Cooper to W. P. Ross, October 21, 1861, in Ross Papers, 61-31, Gilcrease Institute.
33. Order No. 23, October 22, 1861, in Drew Papers, 61-33.
34. *OR*, VIII, 719.

states of Arkansas and Texas were uneasy about the prospect of an open armed revolt among Negroes, free or enslaved. At this time Opothleyahola was thought to have four hundred Negroes under arms, excluding women and children. Knowledge of armed Negroes ignited the fear of slave revolts throughout the Confederacy. The Confederates had visions of women and children behind the lines at the mercy of revolting slaves while their men were away in the Confederate army fighting the Union.

With the exception of two companies that were short of horses, the initial mustering of Drew's regiment was completed on October 30, 1861. The regiment was finally officially mustered into the service of the Confederate States forces at Fort Gibson on November 5, 1861, for a period of twelve months starting on October 25, 1861. The November 5, 1861, muster roll showed 1,214 men enrolled. Their ages ranged from sixteen to seventy-six years. Several Creeks were also listed on the rolls. No whites appeared to be in the roster, although a number of the Cherokees were more than one-half white.[35]

Lieutenant Colonel James J. Diamond of Young's 3d (11th) Texas Regiment, stationed at Fort Gibson, wrote his hometown newspaper in Texas, the Clarksville *Standard*, that "Colonel Drew's Regiment is encamped here, and over one thousand strong of the finest set of warriors that can be found anywhere; they will make their mark wherever they come in contact with the enemy."[36] On the Confederate adjutant and inspector general's official roster, Drew's regiment was initially listed as the 1st Arkansas Mounted Rifles or the 1st Arkansas Cherokee Mounted Rifles. This classification was probably given because the unit was within the jurisdiction of Arkansas. Under Confederate law, following the doctrine of states' rights, the Confederacy could accept military units only from the states. Since the Cherokee Nation was not a state, Arkansas was initially credited with the Indian regiments from the Cherokee Nation. Treaties of friendship and alliance between the Confederate States and various Indian nations along with later amendments to Confederate law soon allowed each Indian Nation to be credited directly for the service of its units. The Indian regiments' association

35. Compiled Service Records of Confederate Soldiers Who Served in Organizations Raised Directly by the Confederate Government, Microcopy 258, roll 77, National Archives Microfilm.
36. Clarksville *Standard* (Texas), November 23, 1861.

with the state of Arkansas was quickly dropped from official correspondence.

With their organization almost completed, Drew's regiment looked forward to taking an active part in the Confederate efforts to protect the Indian nations from Unionists and disloyal elements. Drew's regiment was also to protect Chief John Ross and his followers from Stand Watie and his followers. Instead of the Confederate-Cherokee treaty uniting all Cherokees under one flag and one cause, the formation of two separate Cherokee regiments with loyalty to different political parties and social movements kept the Cherokee Nation divided. What appeared on the surface to be a firm alliance was in fact a hidden chasm.

4
In the Cooweescoowee District

One of the first duties of Colonel John Drew's Regiment of Cherokee Mounted Rifles was carried out when a small detachment was dispatched from Fort Gibson to find and arrest a treasonous horse supplier named Warfield. A letter from Warfield to men named Shaw and Lanigan in Union-held Sante Fe, New Mexico Territory, was intercepted by Confederate authorities. In this letter Warfield offered to sell horses located in Confederate-held territory to the Union army.[1]

Colonel Drew declared that it was his duty to arrest any person communicating with the enemy. In an attempt to find and arrest Warfield, Drew dispatched the small force to the property of R. B. Daniels about sixty miles from Fort Gibson. Although there is no evidence that Warfield was arrested by the regiment, the incident showed the Cherokees that communication with pro-Union authorities and perhaps pro-Union Indians was forbidden and would be dealt with by the Confederacy.[2]

In November, 1861, the Cherokee Nation became increasingly fearful of invasion by the Kansas Jayhawkers, as well as of internal conflicts in the Indian nations because of the presence of Opothleyahola's pro-Union band of loyal Indians from several tribes. Chief John Ross and Colonel John Drew were not anxious to be involved in such a conflict. From Colonel Stand Watie's regiment's camp in the northeastern part of the Cherokee Nation came reports that a thousand Kansas Jayhawkers led by Colonel Charles Rainsford Jennison were preparing to invade the Indian nations. Jennison was the commander of the notorious 7th Kansas Cavalry Regiment, which was well known for its merciless raids on Confederate towns and farms in Missouri. This report caused Cooper to order Drew's regiment to the northern border of the Cherokee Nation to help resist any Union advance.

The loyal, disaffected Indians, led by Opothleyahola, left their

1. J. S. Vann to Cooper, October 30, 1861, in Drew Papers, 61-37.
2. Drew to McCulloch, October 31, 1861, *ibid.*, 61-38.

camp at the junction of the Deep Fork River and the North Fork of the Canadian River on November 5, 1861. Opothleyahola's band slowly headed toward Kansas and a Union fort then being constructed on Walnut Creek. The loyal Indians had finally given up hope of receiving United States representatives or aid. No Union soldiers or agents had ventured into the Indian nations to aid or assure them. Opothleyahola and his followers wanted only to escape harm from the ever-stronger Confederate forces in the Indian nations. The loyal Indians had not yet engaged in any organized acts of aggression against the Confederacy. Women and children, as well as old people, were in Opothleyahola's band with their household goods, furniture, clothes, and food loaded on wagons. The loyal refugees also brought their horses, cattle, and sheep in the exodus. The pro-Union force consisted of about fifteen hundred warriors led by Little Captain, the Creek commander of warriors. About seven hundred Negroes accompanied the loyal Indians. Although some of the Creeks were slaveholders, they had a history of empathy toward Negroes, and fraternization was not uncommon.[3]

A Creek delegation consisting of Oktarharsars Harjo (or Sands), and Mikko Hutke, as well as Seminoles and Chickasaws from Opothleyahola's followers, met with the United States Creek agent George Cutler at LeRoy, Kansas, in November, 1861, to discuss their plight and the need for Federal assistance. This delegation was then sent to Washington, D.C., to plead the Indians' case in person to United States government leaders.[4]

Colonel Cooper sent Colonel Drew a letter on November 10, 1861, ordering the Cherokees to make a "rapid march in the direction of Coody's," or Coody's Bluff, a small Cherokee settlement located where the California Road crossed the Verdigris River in the Cooweescoowee District in the northwest corner of the Cherokee Nation.[5] The California Road was an east–west trail along which many Indians from the Indian nations and people from Missouri and Arkansas had traveled to California during the Gold Rush.

Drew's force was to station itself on the northern fringes of the Cherokee Nation's Cooweescoowee District to cut off a force of Kansas Union raiders reported to be at the Arkansas River in the

3. Trickett, "Civil War in the Indian Territory, 1861," 268–69.
4. Minnie Thomas Bailey, *Reconstruction in Indian Territory: A Story of Avarice, Discrimination and Opportunism* (Port Washington, N.Y., 1972), 33.
5. Cooper to Drew, November 10, 1861, in Drew Papers, 61-39.

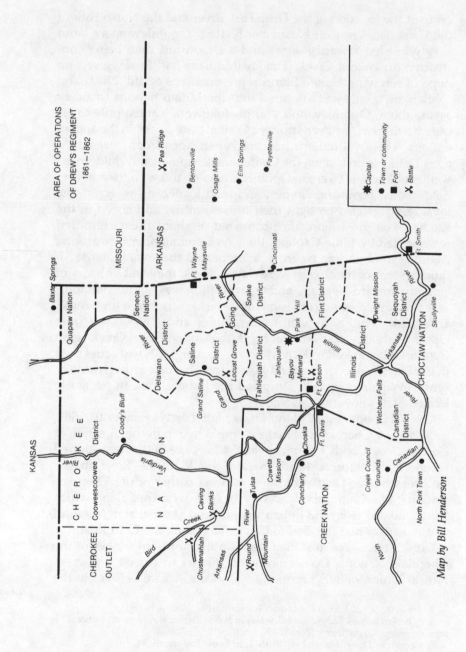

AREA OF OPERATIONS
OF DREW'S REGIMENT
1861–1862

Capital ✹
Town or community ●
Fort ■
Battle ✕

Map by Bill Henderson

southern reaches of the Cooweescoowee District. As soon as the orders to proceed arrived at Drew's regimental headquarters at Fort Gibson, he sent some advance scouts north on the morning of November 12. Drew immediately readied the effective portion of the regiment to march.[6]

Two days later, on November 14, 1861, Colonel Drew and 480 mounted Cherokees galloped up the Verdigris River Valley heading toward Coody's Bluff. Lieutenant Colonel William P. Ross was left at Fort Gibson with about 300 men from various companies in Drew's regiment. These men were the sick, the unarmed, and a few lowly lieutenants who were left to guard the heart of the Cherokee Nation. Nicholas B. Sanders was the only captain from the regiment who was not dispatched to the Cooweescoowee District.[7]

Captain James McDaniel and his reserve company of about fifty men from Drew's regiment were already stationed at McDaniel's home on Hominy Creek in the Cooweescoowee District a few miles from Bird Creek. They named their post Camp McDaniel. McDaniel was a mixed-blood Cherokee politician who had also served as an editor of the *Cherokee Phoenix*.

On November 15, 1861, Colonel Douglas H. Cooper and his command finally marched against Opothleyahola's force, moving up the Deep Fork of the Canadian River. Cooper decided that trying to meet with Opothleyahola was useless and wrote that his overtures of peace were "treated with silence, if not contempt," by Opothleyahola. He also had proof that Opothleyahola was in communication with Federal authorities in Kansas and therefore decided to drive the loyal Indians from the Indian nations before they could cause further mischief. Cooper's Confederate force of about fourteen hundred men consisted of six companies of his 1st Choctaw and Chickasaw Regiment, a detachment of Lieutenant Colonel William Quayle's 9th Texas Cavalry Regiment, Colonel Daniel N. McIntosh's 1st Creek Regiment, Lieutenant Colonel Chilly McIntosh's Creek Battalion, and Major John Jumper's Creek and Seminole Battalion. On reaching the junction of the Deep Fork River and the North Fork of the Canadian River they found that Opothleyahola and his band had already left their old camp and headed north. Rumors in the Indian nations reported that Kansas Jayhawkers were moving south

6. W. P. Ross to Cooper, November 12, 1861, *ibid.*, 61-40.
7. W. P. Ross to Chief Ross, November 16, 1861, in Ross Papers, 61-54, Gilcrease Institute.

to join Opothleyahola in raiding the Confederate elements in the Indian nations. Indeed, pro-Confederate farms were raided and a trading post run by Confederate sympathizer John W. Taylor was burned by the loyal Indians.[8]

On November 16, 1861, Lieutenant Colonel William P. Ross from his camp at Fort Gibson wrote Chief John Ross a note addressed to "Dear Uncle." Lieutenant Colonel Ross proudly reported that about twelve hundred Cherokees had been sworn into service in Drew's regiment. He scornfully wrote, "All the subsistence buildings of the Brigade will pass through the hands of the favored and I have no doubt will be *Privately Contracted* for. I think it probable that the object in wishing to rent that building is to convert it into a Beef packing establishment for individual speculation. It is now occupied by our own Regiment & will be needed for them unless ordered away." Drew's regiment was then storing its supplies in the old commissary store building at Fort Gibson, and Lieutenant Colonel Ross appeared to be concerned about private interests making money by using the old military buildings at Fort Gibson. Dr. Joseph W. Carden, the regiment's assistant surgeon, arrived that evening sick and worn from traveling to Fort Gibson.[9]

Captain James McDaniel, Captain Porum Davis, and Lieutenant Crab Grass Smith operated at Camp McDaniel independently from the regiment in the Cooweescoowee District and were in constant communication with Opothleyahola and his band. Messages received by McDaniel indicated that Opothleyahola wanted only peace and was no real threat to the Cherokee Nation. McDaniel could see no reason to fight Opothleyahola and his followers if they meant no harm to the Cherokee Nation.[10]

Chief John Ross instructed Captain McDaniel in a letter dated November 20, 1861, to escort Opothleyahola safely to Colonel Drew's headquarters at Coody's Bluff or to a home of Chief Ross's brother, Lewis Ross, at the Grand Saline (now known as Salina, Oklahoma) on the Grand or Neosho River. Chief Ross again was trying to come to a peaceful settlement with the loyal Indians.[11]

Unfortunately, the day before Chief Ross sent his message to

8. *OR*, VIII, 5.

9. W. P. Ross to Chief Ross, November 16, 1861, in Ross Papers, 61-54, Gilcrease Institute.

10. *Ibid*.

11. Chief Ross to McDaniel, Porum, and Smith, November 20, 1861, *ibid.*, 61-56.

Captain McDaniel, Colonel Cooper and his force finally caught up with Opothleyahola's band at Round Mountain, west of the Junction of the Cimarron and Arkansas rivers. Cooper's force attacked the loyal Indians, who had their warriors protecting the women, children, and livestock of Opothleyahola's band. Opothleyahola's fighters were led by Creek war chiefs Billy Bowlegs, John Chupco, Halleck Tuskenuggee, and Little Captain. Cooper's force was defeated in the battle, losing 6 killed, 4 wounded, and 1 missing. Cooper reported the loyal Indians' losses as 110 killed and wounded, a figure that appears to be highly inflated. Cooper and his group retreated eastward along the Arkansas River to their wagon train encampment at the small Creek community of Concharty at a wide bend of the Arkansas River.[12]

On the same day as the Battle of Round Mountain, Colonel Drew and his detachment arrived at Coody's Bluff and set up Camp Coody as their base of operations along the Kansas border.[13] Two days later, on Friday, November 22, Colonel Drew and his men received news that a force of 125 Jayhawkers had raided the nearby Cherokee Caney River settlement the previous afternoon. The Kansas raiders captured six or seven Cherokee citizens, including Judge Riley Keyes, the Cooweescoowee District's circuit judge. They had also taken a Negro boy belonging to Joel M. Bryon, a Cherokee rancher, as well as two hundred head of cattle and sixty horses owned by Cherokees.[14]

Within an hour after receiving this news Drew's detachment was on the trail of the Kansas raiders, heading west on the California Road. The avenging Cherokees rode forty miles west of their camp, but to no avail, for after traveling only eighteen miles the Jayhawkers learned from their prisoners that the Cherokee regiment's camp was nearby. The Jayhawkers abandoned the cattle and freed all of their captives except the Negro boy, fleeing north into Kansas. Drew's men followed the Jayhawkers' trail for several days into Kansas, but severe cold weather and the lack of an adequate supply of food forced them to return to Camp Coody. In their haste to overtake the raiders from Kansas, they had not taken sufficient food.[15]

    12. *OR*, VIII, 6.
    13. Drew to Cooper, November 20, 1861, in Drew Papers, 61-41.
    14. Drew to W. P. Ross, November 25, 1861, *ibid.*, 61-43; Drew to Cooper, November 28, 1861, in Foreman Papers, Gilcrease Institute.
    15. Drew to W. P. Ross, November 25, 1861, in Drew Papers, 61-43.

Upon returning to Camp Coody on November 25, Drew and his men learned about the Battle of Round Mountain and Colonel Cooper's defeat. Cooper and his command were still resting and reorganizing at their supply depot at Concharty. Drew expected Cooper to order the Cherokee regiment to join his Confederate Indian and Texan force to continue the pursuit of Opothleyahola's band of loyal Indians.[16]

Camp Coody also received word from Lieutenant Colonel James J. Diamond of the 3d Texas Cavalry Regiment stationed to the east on the Grand River at Lost Creek that another Jayhawker force was in the northeastern corner of the Cherokee Nation. Drew sent more scouts to the south to survey the area between Cooper's forces at Concharty on the Arkansas River and Drew's regiment at Coody's Bluff on the Verdigris River. This scouting party captured a straggler from the group of Jayhawkers that had earlier raided the Cherokee Caney settlement but encountered no other enemy troops.[17]

Colonel Drew also awaited news from Captain McDaniel and other nearby Cherokees concerning Opothleyahola's movements in the Cooweescoowee District. McDaniel in his most recent dispatches to Drew, however, had indicated that his sentiments were with Opothleyahola's band and not with the Confederate pursuers. In fact, the Union Indians of Opothleyahola's force were camped near the supposedly Confederate forces at Camp McDaniel.[18]

Captain McDaniel was ordered to parlay with the loyal Indians to get them to submit to Confederate authorities and send information on their movements to Colonel Drew and Colonel Cooper. McDaniel, however, "always sent a secret message to the Loyal League [Keetoowahs], in the rebel service [Drew's regiment] informing them of his real movements."[19]

Lieutenant Colonel Ross, meanwhile, still at Fort Gibson guarding the Cherokee Nation's main supply depot, was somewhat isolated from invading Jayhawkers and the pro-Union Indians then ravaging the Cherokee Cooweescoowee District. Many members of Drew's regiment were still without adequate arms or were on

16. *Ibid.*
17. Diamond to Drew, November 8, 1861, in Foreman Papers, Gilcrease Institute.
18. Cooper to Drew, November 27, 1861, *ibid.*
19. Delegates of the Cherokee Nation, *Memorial of the Delegates of the Cherokee Nation to the President of the United States and the Senate and House of Representatives in Congress* (Washington, D.C., 1866), 5.

furlough. Among Lieutenant Colonel William P. Ross's three hundred men at least twenty soldiers were incapacitated by an illness that struck the camp at Fort Gibson. Squirrel, a member of Captain Jefferson D. Hicks's Company A, died in the fort of disease on November 22. Lieutenant John Young left the regimental headquarters at Fort Gibson bound for Camp Coody but was forced to return to camp because he was too sick to ride. Those members of the regiment who were not sick wanted to go home instead of sitting out the war guarding stores while Jayhawkers and loyal Indians threatened their homes in the Cherokee Nation.[20]

Frederick A. Kerr, the regimental quartermaster, reported in late November that the commissary building was well stocked with supplies, but most of the regiment was still in the field without access to them. Even in Fort Gibson Kerr heard rumors that Captain James McDaniel and his company in the Cooweescoowee District had deserted and joined Opothleyahola's enemy force. When the Reverend Lewis Downing finally left Fort Gibson, heading for Camp Coody with badly needed supplies, many members of the regiment wanted to accompany him, but only twenty-two men under Captain Sanders were chosen to go with the supply train.[21] Among the necessities that the Reverend Downing's wagons carried was a jug of liquor for a thirsty Colonel John Drew.[22]

From his camp at Spring Hill, just west of the Creek settlement of Concharty, Colonel Cooper sent a scout across the Arkansas River to spy on the Cherokee settlement near Camp McDaniel, where the Locapocka Band of Creek Indians (from what is now Tulsa) was reportedly camped. On November 27, Colonel Cooper reported that his men were fired on by some pro-Union Indians and two of his soldiers were captured and brutally murdered—their brains were knocked out with hominy pestles and their eyes punched out with sticks. Colonel Cooper from his post at Camp Spring Hill strongly denied that his men had encountered and murdered a party of Cherokees, as rumors in the district had reported. On November 27 Colonel Cooper marched in the direction of Tulsey Town or Tulsa with 780 men to overtake and destroy Opothleyahola's followers. Colonel William B. Sims's 9th Texas Cavalry Reg-

20. W. P. Ross to Drew, November 23, 1861, in Foreman Papers, Gilcrease Institute.
21. W. P. Ross to Drew, November 29, 1861, ibid.
22. Kerr to Drew, November 28, 1861, in Drew Papers, 61-44.

iment was also ordered to ride up the Verdigris River toward Coody's Bluff to help trap the Union Indians between the three groups of Confederate troops.[23]

At Tulsey Town on the Arkansas River a prisoner who fled from Opothleyahola's camps was found and questioned by Colonel Cooper's men. The prisoner said a Union Creek force of some two thousand men was planning to attack the Confederates. An alarmed Cooper ordered his men to set up defensive positions immediately and sent orders to Drew and Sims to join forces with him as soon as possible.[24]

Soon after Cooper's scout returned from near Camp McDaniel, rumors again spread throughout the district that Captain James McDaniel and his company had deserted to the enemy. Colonel Drew, trying to verify the rumor, sent a messenger with orders for McDaniel and his men to join the rest of the regiment immediately. Drew's courier returned to Camp Coody with the news that Opothleyahola's force was encamped on the same creek Captain McDaniel lived on, and it appeared that a whole company of Drew's Regiment of Cherokee Mounted Rifles had indeed deserted to the enemy.[25]

23. Cooper to Drew, November 27, 1861, in Foreman Papers, Gilcrease Institute.
24. *OR*, VIII, 7.
25. Cooper to Drew, November 27, 1861, in Foreman Papers, Gilcrease Institute.

5
Disgrace at Caving Banks

The coming of a cold December found Colonel John Drew's detachment of 480 men now located at Camp Brown, still on the northern border of the Cherokee Nation in the Cooweescoowee District. They anxiously awaited news from Captain James McDaniel and his reserve company near Bird Creek. Drew and his men were out of flour, coffee, sugar, and salt and had an inadequate supply of clothes and blankets. They sought additional supplies from the regimental stores at Fort Gibson. It had been many years since the civilized Cherokees had been forced to live strictly off the land. The timely arrival of the Reverend Lewis Downing's supply train from Fort Gibson saved them from starvation in the bitter cold and lifted their spirits.[1]

Colonel Stand Watie, camped on the Grand River, sent a message to Colonel Drew on December 4, 1861, asking for news on the movements of the discontented Creeks and information on any defecting fellow Cherokees. Watie and the rest of the Cherokees were wondering if any more of their Cherokee brothers would follow in Captain McDaniel's footsteps and join Opothleyahola.[2]

As Colonel Drew had long anticipated, orders finally arrived from Colonel Douglas H. Cooper for Drew and his detachment to combine forces "at or near the Crossing of the road leading from David Foreman's on the Verdigris River" to Captain James McDaniel's home. The Cooweescoowee District was so sparsely populated that each farm was a stopover point and an important landmark in a wilderness with few trails. The location of each farm was well known to the Cherokees and travelers through the region. Colonel Cooper's force now consisted of 430 men of the 1st Choctaw and Chickasaw Regiment under Major Mitchell LeFlore, 50 members of Captain Alfred Wade's Choctaw Battalion, 285 men of Colonel Daniel N. McIntosh's 1st Creek Regiment, and 15 Creek scouts led by Captain James M. C. Smith.[3]

1. Drew to W. P. Ross, December 1, 1861, in Foreman Papers, Gilcrease Institute.
2. Watie to Drew, December 4, 1861, in Drew Papers, 61-46.
3. *OR*, VIII, 7.

The men of Drew's regiment accompanying the colonel expected a fight soon. After receiving a letter from his wife carried by Chief John Ross's son, Sergeant Allen Ross, Dr. James P. Evans, the regiment's surgeon, wrote his wife on December 5, 1861, "it is probable that you will hear of fighting in a short time."[4]

Colonel John Drew received news from Opothleyahola's camp that the Loyal Creeks were planning an attack on Cooper's force. Further rumors of an impending attack by the discontented Indians hastened Cooper's desire to combine forces. This union was to occur on Saturday, December 7.[5] Colonel Sims's 9th Texas Cavalry Regiment was to march up the Verdigris River to Mrs. McNair's Place and then join Cooper's command at David Vann's Place. From David Vann's Place, Cooper's enlarged force was to travel north to Musgrove's Place on the Caney River.[6]

On December 6, 1861, Drew's detachment rode out of Camp Brown and traveled twenty-five miles to Cull Vann's Place, which they called Camp Vann. After a fifteen-mile ride the next day, Colonel Drew and his mounted force arrived at Lewis Melton's home on Bird Creek.[7]

Drew's men called their new encampment Camp Melton, but it was not where they were supposed to meet Colonel Cooper and his command. In fact, Drew and his regiment were only six to eight miles northeast of Opothleyahola's camp. Somehow Colonel Drew misunderstood Cooper's orders and marched directly to Melton's home before joining Cooper's force. Thus Drew's regiment with its contingent of Keetoowahs was the first Confederate unit near Opothleyahola's camp twenty-four hours before Cooper had meant for them to arrive. At Camp Melton Drew waited for Cooper and sent out scouts to detect any advancing Union Indians as well as the arrival of Cooper's force.[8]

Lewis Melton, a Cherokee, told Drew's soldiers of the outrages the pro-Union Creeks had recently committed against him and his family. They had destroyed or stolen all of his household goods, ripped open featherbeds, smashed his clock, and killed all his dogs, reportedly just for sport. All of this occurred, he said, because the

4. J. P. Evans to Mrs. Emma I. Evans, December 7, 1861, in Drew Papers, 61-48.
5. Drew to Cooper, December 5, 1861, *ibid.*, 61-47.
6. *OR*, VIII, 7.
7. J. P. Evans to Mrs. Emma I. Evans, December 7, 1861, in Drew Papers, 61-48.
8. *OR*, VIII, 7.

pro-Union Indians lacked shelter in the winter weather and Melton had a warm home to take refuge in. Melton and his family soon fled from the upheaval in the Cooweescoowee District to more tranquil areas in the Cherokee Nation because everyone thought a battle was approaching. After traveling a short distance from Camp Melton, Drew's scouts came into contact with Opothleyahola's forces. Captain George Scraper and some of Drew's men took eight or ten of the Union Indians prisoner in the encounter. Another scouting party under Captain Pickens Benge and Captain Isaac Hildebrand met a party of six to eight Negroes and a few Creeks who asked which side they belonged to. Captain Benge replied that "he belonged to the Cherokee regiment who were soldiers of the South." Outnumbered, Benge and Hildebrand beat a hasty retreat back to the safety of their camp.[9]

On the night of December 7, 1861, at Camp Melton some Keetoowahs of Drew's regiment were on picket or guard duty when Captain James McDaniel approached them and was cordially received. The secret Loyal League held a meeting with McDaniel and the other Keetoowahs in Drew's regiment and planned to desert from the Confederate army; these Cherokees felt they were serving under compulsion. The members of Drew's regiment who were with the Keetoowahs and Loyal League planned to take their guns and ammunition with them when they deserted to Opothleyahola's force.[10]

About noon on December 8, some of Drew's scouts made contact with Colonel Cooper's force near Bird Creek. Knowing the exact location of both Cooper's and Drew's forces, Opothleyahola sent a messenger to Drew at Camp Melton "expressing a desire to make peace." After a conference between Colonel Drew and Colonel Cooper, it was decided that a delegation of Cherokees from Drew's regiment would be sent to meet with Opothleyahola to assure him the Confederacy did not mean them harm and only wanted to settle their differences peacefully. Cooper wanted Drew's Cherokees to tell Opothleyahola they "did not desire the shedding of blood among Indians." At this initial meeting a formal conference would be set up to be held the next day between Colonel Cooper and Opothleyahola. Cooper had been trying to meet with the old Creek

9. J. P. Evans to Mrs. Emma I. Evans, December 7, 1861, in Drew Papers, 61-48.
10. Cherokee Petition to President Lincoln, January 20, 1864, in Cherokee Nation Papers; Delegates of the Cherokee Nation, *Memorial to the President*, 5.

chief for months. At the time of the junction of the Confederate forces, about 1,360 Confederate troops were in the area. Cooper and his men camped on the west side of Bird Creek about two miles south of Drew's Camp Melton and awaited developments. Opothleyahola's camp was reported to be on Bird Creek as close as five miles from Drew's camp.[11]

The peace delegation from Drew's regiment was composed entirely of officers: Major Thomas Pegg, the Reverend Lewis Downing, Captain George W. Scraper, and Captain John Porum Davis. Some of Opothleyahola's men led Drew's delegation to Opothleyahola's camp. These men may have been among the pro-Union Indians Drew's patrol had captured earlier. Only Colonel John Drew and a few junior officers were left in camp to watch over the enlisted Cherokee soldiers. Unknown to the regiment's commander, the Keetoowahs in his command had their own plans for the evening.[12]

With the coming of nightfall a feeling of uneasiness spread among the enlisted men of Drew's regiment. Only half of the full regiment was in camp; the others were either safe at Fort Gibson or in Opothleyahola's camp. The Keetoowah members spread rumors of an impending attack by an overwhelming force of pro-Union Indians. Cooper's forces would be of no assistance in such a surprise attack because they were too far away. Besides, Cooper's force would be attacked, too, the Cherokees reasoned. Following their plan, the Keetoowahs spread panic throughout the regiment. Undoubtedly some of them were in contact with the warriors in Opothleyahola's force.

Unable to bring themselves to fight their brother Keetoowahs already in Opothleyahola's camp, the Keetoowahs in Drew's regiment tied cornhusks in their hair and slipped over to the pro-Union Indians' camp. Reportedly, when two Keetoowahs met, one would ask, "Who are you?" The other would reply with the password, "Tahlequah—who are you?" The proper response was "I am Keetoowah's son."[13]

Colonel Drew, still in camp, soon noticed that a large number of his men were missing. Only about 60 out of his original force of 480 men were in camp. Informed by the remaining soldiers that Opothleyahola's men were about to attack the camp, Drew ordered

11. *OR*, VIII, 7–8.
12. *Ibid.*, 17.
13. Mooney, "Myths of the Cherokees," 226.

his horse saddled and prepared to flee with what was left of his command. While they were preparing to leave, Captain Pickens Benge arrived in camp saying, "We had better be off, as the enemy are upon us." Quickly all the Cherokees mounted their steeds and fled in the direction of Colonel Cooper's camp. But in a comedy of errors, Drew returned to camp with his men to get some ammunition because they had forgotten to take any with them. There they found a confused Major Pegg and the regiment's peace delegation. Benge had given a false alarm, mistaking the approaching delegation for Opothleyahola's warriors.[14]

Captain James Vann of Company E, Captain Albert Pike of Company I, and Captain George W. Scraper of Company G, along with Lieutenants White Catcher, Eli Smith, Samuel Foster, John Bear Meat, and Nathaniel Fish and part of their companies from Drew's regiment already had joined Opothleyahola's camp that night. Also in the Union Indians' camp were Captain James McDaniel and Lieutenants Watt Stop, Noah Drowning Bear, and Big Sky yah too kah (Skieyaltooka) from McDaniel's company, which had deserted previously.[15] In all some six hundred Cherokee soldiers from Drew's regiment would desert and join Opothleyahola's loyal Indians.[16]

Major Pegg reported to Colonel Drew that Opothleyahola's four thousand men were painted for battle and planning to attack that night. The peace party from Drew's command said they had been allowed to leave the Union Indians' camp only after pleading that they wanted to remove some women and children from danger. This was, of course, false, for there were no women or children in Drew's camp. There had been no peace conference between Pegg's Cherokees and the loyal Indians as planned. Major Pegg's group had not even been allowed to see Opothleyahola. The meeting had been a ruse to get the officers loyal to Chief Ross and the Confederacy out of camp so most of the regiment could desert to the Union Indians' camp without a fight. The ruse had succeeded beyond all expectations. It was now dark, and the panicked Cherokees from Drew's regiment who were still loyal to the Confederacy broke into small parties to try to break through the ring of Opothleyahola's warriors that they believed were surrounding the camp. With their tents still standing, the bewildered remnants of Drew's regiment

14. *OR*, VIII, 7–8.
15. *Ibid*.
16. Delegates of the Cherokee Nation, *Memorial to the President*, 5.

sneaked out of camp again, leaving behind horses, guns, and most of their camp equipment.[17]

Colonel Cooper's first news of the disaster among Drew's regiment came when a few Cherokee stragglers appeared in Cooper's camp at about seven o'clock in the evening. The Cherokees reported that Major Pegg had been unsuccessful in the conference and Opothleyahola was preparing to attack Cooper's camp. Colonel Cooper was also informed that Drew's regiment had fled from the camp. These stragglers were soon followed by Drew's regimental wagon master and his teamsters along with a few of their wagons and some of the regiment's ammunition and supplies. Cooper quickly alerted his entire force to protect the camp from the expected attack by Opothleyahola's army.[18]

A squadron from the 9th Texas Cavalry Regiment under Lieutenant Colonel William Quayle left Cooper's camp to scout Drew's camp and provide assistance to the Cherokees if possible. Colonel Cooper expected Drew's men to be defending their camp from the Union Indians. Quayle's cavalry ran into Colonel Drew and what was left of his command and escorted the confused men back to Drew's abandoned camp. The Cherokees and Texans secured the rest of the Cherokees' baggage train, tents, and other necessary equipment. Still there was no sign of Opothleyahola's warriors. The Texans escorted the remnant of Drew's regiment to Cooper's camp. Only twenty-eight Cherokees managed to find their way to the Confederate main body with Colonel Drew. Drew and his few men aided Cooper's men in preparing the Confederate camp to defend against the expected attack.[19]

Other Cherokees later straggled into Cooper's camp, but most deserted to Opothleyahola's camp or fled southeastward toward Fort Gibson. Major Thomas Pegg, Adjutant James S. Vann, Captain John Porum Davis, Captain Jefferson D. Hicks, Lieutenant Samuel H. Smith, Lieutenant Jesse Henry, Lieutenant Anderson Benge, Lieutenant Trotting Wolf, and several of the regiment's enlisted men fled toward Fort Gibson, making no effort to join Cooper's force. Cooper later reported that Drew could gather only seventy men of his regiment at Cooper's camp after that disastrous night. Without a shot being fired, Cooper's Confederate force had lost about one-

17. *OR*, VIII, 7–8.
18. *Ibid.*, 8.
19. *Ibid.*

third of its men. Some of these same soldiers were new additions to Opothleyahola's force.[20]

There was an all-night vigil at Cooper's camp with the Confederate force awaiting attack, but no attack came, or even the hint of an enemy. At daybreak a party of soldiers led by Adjutant Roswell W. Lee scouted Drew's camp and found it still untouched. No enemy was in sight. Upon receiving this information from Lee, Colonel Cooper sent the remains of Drew's command, some Texas cavalry, and a few Choctaws to Camp Melton, where the rest of the regimental equipment was recovered. Captain Abram Foster and two Creek companies left Cooper's camp on the morning of December 9 to scout in the direction of Park's Store on Shoal Creek to see if Opothleyahola's warriors had come down from their camps in the hills to the west. The Confederate Creek patrol under Captain Foster was also searching for Captain Robert C. Parks and his patrol, which had not been seen since they had left Cooper's camp the previous night to scout Opothleyahola's camp. Additional Confederate reinforcements were expected to join Cooper's force by way of Tulsey Town or Tulsa to the south and Cooper's depot at Coweta Mission to the southeast. Cooper's force broke camp and crossed over to the east side of Bird Creek to maintain communications with their depot at Coweta Mission, a church located on the north side of the Arkansas River about five miles north of Concharty and just southeast of Tulsey Town.[21]

Cooper's force had marched about five miles south along Bird Creek when two runners from Captain Foster's scouting party arrived with the news that the two Confederate Creek companies had run into a large force of Union Indians and traded shots with them. In the firefight Captain Parks and his men, who had been found by Foster's men, captured six of the Union Indians and withdrew toward Cooper's force. Shooting then commenced at the rear guard of Cooper's column when another Union Indian force attacked about two miles from a horseshoe bend on Bird Creek.[22]

Drew's baggage train, parked on the prairie, was put under the protection of some of his command, and Cooper ordered the Confederate soldiers to skirmish with the Union Indians along Bird Creek. Drew's detachment of Cherokees was placed with the Texans

20. *Ibid.*, 17, 709.
21. *Ibid.*, 8.
22. *Ibid.*, 8, 19.

in the center of the attacking Confederate column, with the 1st Choctaw and Chickasaw Regiment on the right and the 1st Creek Regiment on the left. Colonel Cooper did not have much confidence in the loyalty or fighting ability of the remaining Cherokees under Colonel Drew in the upcoming battle. The Confederate column galloped toward the Union Indians along a two-mile line in the timber and ravines of the prairie along Bird Creek.[23]

Among Opothleyahola's warriors fighting the advancing Confederates were Cherokees who only recently had been in Drew's Confederate regiment, which they were now fighting against. Some 430 soldiers and 4 captains from Drew's regiment, including Captain James McDaniel's company, were among those now shooting at Cooper's advancing cavalry. Most pro-Union Cherokees were armed with guns and ammunition taken from the regiment's camp the previous night.[24]

While the three lines of Confederates made a frontal attack across the prairie against the Union Indians, a force of some 200 Union Indians attacked the Confederate rear guard. Captain Young's Choctaw and Chickasaw Squadron protected the rear guard and drove the attackers back into the woods. Two companies of the 1st Choctaw and Chickasaw Regiment and all of the 1st Creek Regiment proceeded along the edge of Bird Creek. Colonel Drew and his men fought beside the Confederate Choctaws, Chickasaws, and Texans in an attempt to clear out the Union Indians hidden in the ravines on the east bank of Bird Creek. On the prairie the rest of the 1st Choctaw and Chickasaw Regiment and the Texans made a mad charge, driving the Union Indians from a big ravine on the open prairie and chasing them into the woods along Bird Creek.[25]

The main body of Opothleyahola's warriors was centered at a horseshoe bend on the west side of muddy Bird Creek at a place known to the Cherokees as Chusto-Talash or Caving Banks and to the Creeks as Fonta-hulwache or Little High Shoals. The horseshoe bend was a formidable bastion of steep riverbanks, fords known only to the defenders, and a small farm in the center of the bend. Logs piled high around a log cabin, a corn crib, and a fence provided protection for the Union Indians on the west side of the creek in the center of the bend and served as their central defense point. For-

23. *Ibid.*, 8.
24. Petition to President Lincoln, January 20, 1864, in Cherokee Nation Papers.
25. *OR*, VIII, 8–9.

tification of this horseshoe bend was typical of traditional Creek battle tactics; for hundreds of years they had used horseshoe bends in rivers and creeks as natural defenses in battles or for the protection of their towns. A gorge in the prairie was located to the west of the bend in an old stream cut, and here some of the Union Indians sought protection as the Confederate cavalry crossed over to the west side of Bird Creek north of the horseshoe bend and began its attack. On the south end of the horseshoe bend was a series of shoals with forty-to-fifty-foot-high sandstone bluffs on the east bank of Bird Creek in some places. The horseshoe bend covered about a quarter of a mile and Bird Creek itself presented an obstacle for the Confederates to cross to reach the Union defenses.[26]

The Texans of Cooper's brigade led the attack on the Union forces on the east bank of Bird Creek with the Creek regiment sweeping the Union Indians farther east in the prairie. For several hours the battle raged in close-quarter combat as flanking movements and quick assaults by the Confederates brought them into direct contact with the Union Indians. The Confederates were often forced to dismount and fight on foot. Lieutenant Colonel Quayle's Texans advanced to the left of the 1st Choctaw and Chickasaw Regiment while Colonel Sims led his force to the right of the 1st Creek Regiment. The Texans moved about one mile down the east bank of Bird Creek sweeping the disorganized Union Indians before them. About one hundred Choctaws and Chickasaws of Captain Young's company crossed over to the west bank of Bird Creek and charged the house located in the middle of the strategic horseshoe bend, capturing it. The Choctaws and Chickasaws then dismounted and fought on foot, while parts of three additional Choctaw and Chickasaw companies crossed to the west side of Bird Creek to reinforce Young's company at the house. This force succeeded in placing the Union Indians in a crossfire. Part of the Union Indians crossed over to the east side of Bird Creek, moved north along the east bank, and began to fire on the Choctaws and Chickasaws gathered around the house in the horseshoe bend. The Union Indians still in the horseshoe bend rallied and attacked, forcing the Confederates back to the house, and the fight seesawed back and forth for thirty minutes. Another group of Union Indians attempted to circle around and capture the Confederates' horses, but the Confederates noticed the

26. Petition to President Lincoln, January 20, 1864, in Cherokee Nation Papers.

flanking movement and rushed troops to cut off the attack, forcing the Union Indians to retreat. McIntosh's Creek regiment then joined the 1st Choctaw and Chickasaw Regiment at the horseshoe bend, and these fresh troops finally drove the Union Indians across the bend.[27]

The Confederates also drove the rest of Opothleyahola's men across the prairie from the ravines and protected riverbanks. About dark, after four hours of combat, an estimated twenty-five hundred to four thousand Union warriors withdrew to their scattered camps in the Osage Hills to the northwest, where their women and children were located. The exhausted Confederate force likewise withdrew to its camp since most of the ammunition each rider had carried into the fight was depleted. The Confederate wagons were loaded with wounded and taken to Vann's Place under an escort led by Colonel Sims. The next day, after replenishing their ammunition from the supply wagons, Cooper's brigade returned to the site of the battle only to find the Union Indians had gone, leaving behind their dead. Cooper's brigade lost fifteen killed and thirty-seven wounded in the Battle of Caving Banks. In Drew's regiment, at least on the Confederate side, Lieutenant Broom Baldridge was killed and Captain Richard Fields had his horse shot out from under him during the fight.[28]

Although Colonel Douglas H. Cooper reported that the loyal Indians had lost at least 500 killed and wounded, the actual loyal Indian losses were probably better represented by the 27 bodies found by Cooper's men and an estimated 200 to 300 wounded who escaped. Colonel Cooper reported that captured Union Indians later tallied their losses at 412, but this figure seems highly inflated. In a skirmishing battle with most of the fighting taking place from behind the cover of trees and in ravines, the actual losses to the Union Indians could not be well documented. Cooper's men buried the dead on the battlefield and returned to the brigade's wagon train still parked at Vann's Place. The following members of Drew's regiment fought on the Confederate side at the Battle of Caving Banks: Company D, Captain Isaac N. Hildebrand, Lieutenant George Springston, Lieutenant Ezekiel Russell, and Private Nelson

27. *OR*, VIII, 9–10.
28. *Ibid.*, 10.

Hogshooter; Company F, Captain Richard Fields, Lieutenant Broom Baldridge, Sergeant Dempsey Handle, Private Creek Mc-Coy, Private Situwakee, and Private Tracker; Company H, Captain Edward R. Hicks, Lieutenant George W. Ross, Sergeant William Hewbanks, Sergeant Allen Ross, Sergeant Peter, Private Henry Meigs, Private Richard Robinson, Private Carter Oo yor lor choo he, and Private Coming Deer; Company K, Captain Pickens M. Benge, Lieutenant George Benge, Private Oliver Ross, Private Thomas Ross, Private Broad Christy, Private Thomas Yay hoo lar, and Private Adams (a Creek); and regimental staff, Colonel John Drew, Surgeon James P. Evans, and Expressman William S. Coody.[29] Clearly, Chief John Ross's sons did not desert, nor did any other of his direct relations. Among the Cherokees it appears that family bonds were extremely dependable in times of crisis.

The day before the Battle of Caving Banks, Lieutenant Colonel William P. Ross led part of Drew's regiment from Fort Gibson to join the rest of the regiment on Bird Creek to aid Cooper's brigade in the expected fight with Opothleyahola's band. This force was part of the reinforcements expected by Cooper. Drew's regiment at Fort Gibson consisted of probably about three hundred men, mostly unarmed, with the following officers: Lieutenant Colonel William P. Ross, Captain Nicholas B. Sanders, Lieutenant George O. Sanders, Lieutenant Lacy Hawkins, Lieutenant Ah mer cher ner, Lieutenant Crab Grass Smith, Lieutenant Fogg, Lieutenant Little Bird, Lieutenant John Young, Lieutenant William Webber, Lieutenant Samuel Downing, Lieutenant Charles Drew, Lieutenant Ulteesky, Lieutenant Deer in the Water Star, and Assistant Surgeon Joseph Carden.[30]

On the road from Fort Gibson to Camp Melton Lieutenant Colonel Ross and his men encountered some of the officers and men who had fled from Camp Melton on the night of the peace mission. The terrified Cherokees from Drew's camp brought reports of the wholesale desertion of their fellow Cherokees from Drew's detachment to Opothleyahola's forces. The disorganized soldiers also reported that the Union Indians had an overwhelming superiority in forces. It was likely, they thought, that even Colonel Cooper's brigade might have been surrounded and wiped out. Lieutenant Colonel Ross, not wishing to fight fellow Cherokees or to ride into a trap,

29. *Ibid.*, 10, 16, 17.
30. *Ibid.*

decided discretion was the better part of valor and beat a hasty
retreat to Fort Gibson with all that remained, as far as he knew, of
Drew's Cherokee regiment, to await events.[31]

Although the Battle of Caving Banks was considered to be a Confederate victory, the disintegration and desertion of much of Drew's
regiment made it a hollow victory. Opothleyahola and his band of
loyal followers still remained in the hills and valleys in the Cherokee
Cooweescoowee District presenting an unsettling influence among
the Cherokees and any loyal Indians not yet in their band. A major
rift had also appeared among the Cherokees, as the Ross party was
now split into a Union and a Confederate faction.

31. W. P. Ross to Chief Ross, December 9, 1861, in Ross Papers, 61-59, Gilcrease
Institute.

6
Licking Their Wounds

On arriving at Vann's Place on the night of December 10, the weary Confederate troops were greeted by dismal news. On the same day as the Battle of Caving Banks a force of one hundred Cherokees from Fort Gibson had put on the "shuck badge" or cornhusks and joined Opothleyahola at his camp on Shoal Creek. Some of these Cherokees were probably part of Lieutenant Colonel William P. Ross's command from Fort Gibson, which had earlier met survivors fleeing from Camp Melton.[1]

To prevent more Cherokees from joining the Union Indians, Colonel Drew left Vann's Place bound for Fort Gibson with his remaining men and supplies. He was accompanied by Colonel Sims's 9th Texas Cavalry Regiment. At the same time Colonel Cooper and his brigade rode through Tulsey Town or Tulsa and camped at Choska on December 13, 1861, to block additional Union Indian reinforcements coming from the south. The rapid deterioration of events in the Cherokee Nation led Colonel Cooper to write to Colonel James McIntosh on December 11, 1861, requesting immediate aid from Confederate troops stationed in Arkansas. Confederate strength in the Indian nations no longer was adequate to ensure that the pro-Union Indians would not gain superiority. Quick action was needed to prevent more pro-Union Indians from joining Opothleyahola and possibly taking control of Indian Territory. The split among the Cherokees made it likely that most of the Cherokee Nation might come under Union control.[2]

The desertion of a large portion of Drew's regiment caused the Confederate white troops to doubt the future performance of the Indians. One Texan wrote, "I do not like to fight with the Indians very much, for you do not know at what moment they will turn over to the opposite side, and if you get in a fight with them and the enemy pours in a pretty heavy fire, they will go away with them."[3]

1. *OR*, VIII, 11.
2. *Ibid.*, 11, 709.
3. Letter of December 16, 1861, in *Texas Republican* (Washington, Texas), January 4, 1862.

Colonel John Drew and Colonel William B. Sims brought the news of the Confederate victory at Caving Banks to Fort Gibson. This news halted more mass desertions to the Union Indian camps. Colonel Cooper marched down along the Arkansas River with Welch's Texas Squadron and a few companies of the 1st Choctaw and Chickasaw Regiment a few days after Drew's force arrived at Fort Gibson. Cooper's detachment camped across the Grand River from Fort Gibson while the rest of his brigade remained at Choska. Chief John Ross, Colonel John Drew, and Colonel Douglas H. Cooper conferred on the necessity of the Cherokees living up to their treaty with the Confederate States. In Arkansas Colonel James McQueen McIntosh received urgent requests for reinforcements from Colonel Cooper, and he ordered Confederate troops stationed in Arkansas to march to Fort Gibson to suppress the Union Indian uprising. He also allowed additional ammunition to be dispatched to the Indian nations from Confederate supplies in Arkansas.[4]

To the northeast of Fort Gibson, near Captain Albert Pike's house in Tahlequah, some three hundred Cherokees who had recently deserted from Drew's regiment gathered to discuss their dilemma. Accompanying this group of deserters on December 16, 1861, were Captain James Vann, Captain Albert Pike, and Captain George W. Scraper. The Cherokee deserters sent a delegation to Chief John Ross in an attempt to make peace with their Cherokee brothers who still honored the treaty with the Confederacy. The deserters from Drew's regiment had no wish to fight their friends and relatives still loyal to the Confederacy, but they also had no desire to fight Watie's men. Drew reported that "members of my Regiment who have been out are coming in not very fast."[5]

Chief John Ross still wanted to prevent a civil war among his people. He forgave those who deserted from Drew's regiment and promised them amnesty. Many pro-Confederate Cherokees, especially members of Watie's regiment, were unforgiving and were enraged by Ross's leniency to the Cherokee deserters. By all the rules of warfare they should have been shot, but Chief Ross did not have it in his heart to punish those of his followers who had acted on their convictions and sided with Opothleyahola. The gap between Ross's and Watie's factions widened. Dissent even divided Chief Ross's followers within the Ross party.

4. *OR*, VIII, 11.
5. Drew to Chief Ross, December 16, 1861, in Foreman Papers, Gilcrease Institute.

On December 19, 1861, Chief John Ross spoke to the remainder of Drew's regiment at Fort Gibson. Speaking in Cherokee, Ross said: "A few nights ago I had occasion to address some of you on a very strange and extraordinary occasion, and now that you are nearly all present, I will necessarily have to repeat much that I then said. I then told you of the difficulty caused in the nation by the disruption of the United States, and the action taken by our neighboring States and tribes in joining the southern confederacy, which had left us alone, and of other matters of equal interest, that made it necessary for us to call a convention of the Cherokee people." He went on to review the circumstances that led the Cherokees to sign a treaty with the Confederacy and to remind the Cherokees of their duties and obligations to that treaty.[6]

Colonel Douglas H. Cooper then addressed Drew's regiment stressing the need to remain loyal to the Confederacy and to uphold their honor. Major Thomas Pegg also spoke to the soldiers in Cherokee on the necessity of remaining loyal to their new treaty with the Confederacy. Cooper then ordered the immediate reorganization of Drew's regiment, for as an effective fighting force it was almost nonexistent. About one-half of the regiment had deserted or resigned, and the remainder was demoralized by the recent events. After agreeing with Colonel Drew and Chief John Ross on the regiment's reorganization, Cooper returned to his camp at the Creek village of Choska and left orders for Drew's reorganized regiment to join him when possible. Nevertheless, some members of the regiment left for their homes, having no desire to fight Opothleyahola or show their approval of the treaty with the Confederate States of America.[7]

Chief John Ross allowed some of the deserters from Drew's regiment who had fought against their own regiment to resign their commissions. James S. Vann, adjutant of Drew's regiment, tendered his resignation on December 20, 1861, at Fort Gibson. None of the deserters, however, appear to have been punished by Chief John Ross, the Cherokee government, or the Confederacy.[8]

On December 29, 1861, Colonel James McQueen McIntosh with sixteen hundred Texas and Arkansas cavalry from General Ben McCulloch's army at winter camp near Van Buren, Arkansas, arrived at

6. Joseph Thoburn (ed.), "The Cherokee Question," *Chronicles of Oklahoma*, II (March, 1924), 185–88.

7. *OR*, VIII, 12.

8. Vann to Drew, December 20, 1861, in Foreman Papers, Gilcrease Institute.

Fort Gibson. McIntosh announced his intention to take his command into the field immediately against Opothleyahola and the Union Indians. Colonel James M. McIntosh was the son of Colonel James S. McIntosh, who had served in the United States Army and was killed during the Mexican War. James M. McIntosh graduated from West Point in 1849, was a captain in the 1st United States Cavalry Regiment, and served at Fort Arbuckle and Fort Cobb in Indian Territory as well as at Fort Smith, Arkansas. On May 7, 1861, he resigned his United States Army commission and joined the 2d Arkansas Mounted Rifles Regiment as its colonel. Colonel McIntosh and his force of white troops were welcome additions to the Confederate forces trying to chase Opothleyahola and his band from the Indian nations.[9]

In spite of Brigadier General Albert Pike's assertion that Drew's men were eager to fight against "the Yankees; but did not wish to fight their own brethren, the Creeks," most of the Confederate command considered Drew's regiment useless as a fighting force. The regiment was reorganized with a few officers and soldiers added to replace some of those who had deserted, but it was severely reduced in strength. After a number of soldiers were raised in rank to replace the officers and noncommissioned officers who had deserted, Drew's regiment joined Cooper's brigade at Choska.[10]

Colonel James McIntosh's force left Fort Gibson at noon on December 22, 1861, with five companies of Lieutenant Colonel Walter P. Lane's 3d Texas (South Kansas–Texas) Cavalry Regiment, Lieutenant Colonel John S. Griffith's 6th Texas Cavalry Regiment, seven companies of Colonel W. C. Young's 3d (11th) Texas Cavalry Regiment, four companies of Colonel James M. McIntosh's 2d Arkansas Mounted Rifles, and Captain H. S. Bennett's Lamar (Texas) Cavalry Company. True to his word, McIntosh thoroughly crushed Opothleyahola's force on Hominy Creek in the Cherokee Cooweescoowee District in the Battle of Chustenahlah or Patriot Hills on December 26, 1861, just a few miles northwest of the site of the Battle of Caving Banks.

McIntosh's force defeated the Union Indians without any direct aid from Colonel Cooper because Cooper's teamsters had deserted and his brigade was delayed at McNair's Place. In the battle McIn-

9. OR, VIII, 11.
10. Annie Heloise Abel, *The American Indian as Participant in the Civil War* (Cleveland, 1919), 138.

tosh's force suffered 8 killed and 32 wounded. He reported that over 250 of Opothleyahola's followers were killed and 160 women and children, 20 Negroes, 30 wagons, 70 yoke of oxen, 500 horses, several hundred cattle, 100 sheep, and other goods were captured. Captain James McDaniel, formerly of Drew's regiment, missed the massacre because he was in Kansas seeking Federal aid for the Union Indians in the Indian nations. As Opothleyahola's followers broke into small bands of men, women, and children trying to flee into Kansas, the Confederate forces pursued them. Just as the battle ended, Colonel Stand Watie's regiment arrived on the scene from its post on the Grand River and joined McIntosh's forces in chasing the defeated loyal Indians. Watie's regiment killed and captured another 100 Union Indians without any losses in a series of running fights twenty to twenty-five miles from the site of the Battle of Patriot Hills. Colonel Douglas H. Cooper also arrived with his Indian Brigade after the main battle and helped pursue the demoralized and frantic Union Indian survivors.[11]

The weather was intensely cold. A sleet storm on January 1, 1862, enabled the Confederate trackers to follow several fleeing bands of Union Indians. Their trails generally led north toward Walnut Creek in Kansas. Colonel Cooper's force headed southward to the Arkansas River. Upon its arrival at the battlefield of Patriot Hills, Drew's regiment was ordered to follow a trail left by some Union Indian wagons. Drew's regiment soon came upon a small Union Cherokee camp and attacked it. Several loyal Cherokees were captured, and one was wounded in the fight. After the skirmish Drew's regiment stopped its pursuit of the fleeing Union Indians and headed toward Cooper's camp. At Skiatooka's Settlement on the Great Bend of the Arkansas River (near present Keystone Lake) Drew's regiment stopped and obtained some badly needed meat and corn. With the rest of Cooper's brigade, Drew's regiment reached Tulsey Town on January 4, 1862, where a Confederate supply train was waiting with food and supplies. Cooper's brigade had made a forced march of several days over mostly uninhabited country in pursuit of the Union Indians and had killed 6 and captured 150 pro-Union Indians, mostly women and children.[12]

While on the way back to camp on the Grand River with 800 to 900 head of cattle and 250 ponies captured from Opothleyahola's band,

11. *OR*, VIII, 12–13, 22–33.
12. *Ibid.*, 12–13.

two companies of Watie's regiment were sent to arrest a company of fifty to sixty armed pro-Union Cherokees nearby. These loyal Cherokees had two wagons and were heading north to join other Union Indians near the Kansas border when they passed near Watie's camp. Watie's two companies halted them, and a fight developed in which Watie's men killed one, captured seven, and scattered the rest. Watie's men also captured the loyal Cherokees' wagons. Once again Colonel Stand Watie demonstrated that his men were not afraid to kill fellow Cherokees who sided with the Union. In fact, they seemed to relish obtaining revenge against their brethren.[13]

Drew's regiment returned to camp near Tahlequah while Watie's regiment was stationed on the northern border of the Cherokee Nation, poised to confront any Union scouting parties or fleeing pro-Union Indians. The two units were generally kept separated to prevent bloodshed because of their intense hatred for each other. Although the Cherokees had been in Confederate service for several months, they still had not received any pay for their services. The lack of hard cash, which had been promised by the treaty, increased dissatisfaction in Drew's command. On December 31, 1861, the Confederate Congress approved an act providing that for Drew's regiment an "allowance in lieu of clothing shall be paid only to such of said officers and men as . . . mustered into service, and that none shall be paid who have deserted or disbanded without permission, or have taken sides with the insurrectionists among the Creeks."[14]

Opothleyahola gathered survivors of his army at Roe's Fort on the Verdigris River in Kansas about fifteen miles south of the town of Belmont on Indian land on which white settlers were prohibited. Some eight to ten thousand pro-Union Indians, many destitute, sick, and without clothing and shelter, huddled in camp awaiting supplies from the United States government. Only the strong would survive the winter.

Hatred intensified between the two factional Cherokee regiments during the winter. An example of this distrust is found in a February 19, 1862, letter from Colonel Stand Watie to Colonel Douglas H. Cooper. While on a scout, two of Watie's men apprehended Arch Snail, a member of Captain Isaac N. Hildebrand's Company D of Drew's regiment. Arch Snail, like some other Cherokees still in

13. *Ibid.*, 31.
14. *Ibid.*, Ser. IV, Vol. I, pp. 821–22.

Drew's regiment, had deserted at Caving Banks but had later rejoined the regiment. Snail was being led back to Watie's camp when several of his campanions from Drew's regiment were reported to have ambushed the patrol of Watie's men. Watie wrote, "Snail was killed with his own pistol. As to the other two assassins I know nothing of them, but presume that they are safe in Col. Drew's Camps."[15]

Another deserter from Drew's regiment, Chunestootie, was killed and scalped by Colonel Stand Watie's nephew Charles Webber. Webber was the best friend of Saladin Watie, Stand Watie's oldest son. Chunestootie was a member of Captain Ross's company of Drew's regiment and at the time he was killed was said to be "beside himself with liquor." Colonel Watie regretted the incident, but he wrote that Chunestootie had been "hostile to southern people and their institutions" and had been one of the party who had vowed to kill "any and all who should attempt to raise a southern flag." Colonel Drew called the action a crime that shocked his command, but because of the turbulent times no effort was made to punish the murderer. Such incidents, however, only increased old hatreds in the Cherokee Nation because the laws were not being enforced.[16]

Conflict between the two Confederate Cherokee Indian regiments prevented them from cooperating in the Cherokee Nation. In fact, the members of Drew's regiment had two enemies, the Union and Watie's regiment.

15. Edward Everett Dale and Gaston Litton (eds.), *Cherokee Cavaliers: Forty Years of Cherokee History as Told in the Correspondence of the Ridge-Watie-Boudinot Family* (Norman, 1939), 113.
16. *Ibid.*, 112.

Rose Cottage, Chief John Ross's home at Park Hill
Western History Collections, University of Oklahoma Library

Chief John Ross
The Thomas Gilcrease Institute of American History and Art, Tulsa, Oklahoma

Colonel John Drew, commander of Drew's Regiment of Cherokee Mounted Rifles
Archives and Manuscripts Division, Oklahoma Historical Society

Colonel Stand Watie, leader of the Ridge party and commander of Watie's regiment
Western History Collections, University of Oklahoma Library

The Reverend John B. Jones, Baptist abolitionist, cofounder of the Keetoowahs, and chaplain of the 2d Kansas Indian Home Guard Regiment
Archives and Manuscripts Division, Oklahoma Historical Society

Israel Vore, quartermaster of Drew's regiment
Bureau of American Ethnology

Brigadier General Albert Pike, Indian commissioner of the lands west of Arkansas
and commander of the Confederate Indian Brigade
Archives and Manuscripts Division, Oklahoma Historical Society

Chief Opothleyahola, leader of the Loyal Creeks, in 1838
Archives and Manuscripts Division, Oklahoma Historical Society

Colonel Douglas H. Cooper, commander of the 1st Choctaw and Chickasaw Regiment

Archives and Manuscripts Division, Oklahoma Historical Society

Colonel Daniel N. ("Dode") McIntosh, commander of the 1st Creek Regiment and leader of the Confederate Creeks
Archives and Manuscripts Division, Oklahoma Historical Society

Fanciful 1889 Kurtz and Allison print of the capture of the Union battery near Leetown by Cherokees and Texans during the Battle of Pea Ridge

The Thomas Gilcrease Institute of American History and Art, Tulsa, Oklahoma

Confederate Cherokee delegates at Washington, D.C., at the end of the Civil War. From left to right: John Rollin Ridge, Saladin Ridge Watie (Stand Watie's son), Richard Fields (formerly of Drew's regiment), Elias Cornelious Boudinot, and William Penn Adair

Courtesy University of Oklahoma Press and Archives and Manuscripts Division, Oklahoma Historical Society

7

The Pea Ridge Campaign

Uneasiness continued in the Cherokee Nation; the Indians were now as divided as any border state. In addition, large Union armies in Kansas and Missouri were on the move. Although the weakly defended Cherokee Nation was within easy reach, the Union armies were after much bigger game. On Christmas Day, 1861, Brigadier General Samuel Ryan Curtis assumed command of the Federal Southwestern District of Missouri and began planning to drive the Confederates from Missouri into Arkansas. Curtis was born in 1807 near Champlain, New York, graduated from West Point in 1831, served as second lieutenant in the 7th United States Infantry Regiment, and was assigned to Fort Gibson in the Cherokee Nation. He resigned from the United States Army in 1832 to become a lawyer and civil engineer. During the Mexican War he served as lieutenant colonel of the 3d Ohio Volunteer Infantry Regiment. After the war, Curtis moved to Iowa, where he practiced law, then became engineer in charge of St. Louis, Missouri, served as chief engineer to the American Central Railroad, and completed several terms in Congress as a Republican from Iowa. On June 1, 1861, Curtis became commander of the 2d Iowa Volunteer Infantry Regiment and was soon commissioned as a brigadier general.[1]

In an unusual winter campaign General Curtis' Union army chased Major General Sterling Price's Confederate army of Missouri State Guards (militia) from Springfield, Missouri, before Confederate forces led by Brigadier General Ben McCulloch at winter camps in Missouri and Arkansas could come to Price's assistance. The failure of the Confederates to oppose Curtis was owing to the intense dislike between the two senior Confederate officers in the region, Price and McCulloch. Each operated his command independently of the other. This antagonism between commanders enabled the Union forces to take control of southwestern Missouri with little effort because they met no cooperative resistance.

1. Captain A. A. Stuart, *Iowa Colonels and Regiments: Being a History of Iowa Regiments in the War of the Rebellion* (Des Moines, 1865), 35–36.

Major General Earl Van Dorn was assigned as the commander of the newly created Confederate Trans-Mississippi District of Department No. 2 on January 10, 1862, to ease the tension between Price and McCulloch. Van Dorn, a commander acceptable to all the Confederate units, was ordered to unify the forces in Missouri and western Arkansas. He called his new command the Army of the West.

In mid-February, 1862, Price's Missouri militia was chased into northwestern Arkansas by General Curtis' Union army. Major General Van Dorn ordered McCulloch and Price to join forces with all available Confederate units in the Army of the West to drive the invading Union army back into Missouri. On February 25, 1862, Van Dorn sent orders to Brigadier General Albert Pike to move immediately with his Indian brigade to Bentonville, Arkansas, to join McCulloch and Price in the march against the Union invaders.

On February 25, 1862, Pike had about $500,000 in cash, including $96,000 in gold, at Cantonment Davis, where he had just arrived to explain recent changes in their treaties with the Confederacy to various Indian tribes. The funds were to pay the reserve Indians, which included the Osages and Comanches, the money due them by treaties. The members of the 1st Choctaw and Chickasaw Regiment, as well as the 1st Creek Regiment, also demanded payment of the funds due them for their military service and declared that if they were not paid they would not accompany Pike to fight the Union forces in Arkansas. Pike tried to explain that he was paying treaty money to the Indian tribes and could not use these funds for army pay. Because of the extreme need for the Indian troops in the coming Arkansas campaign Pike was forced to pay the Choctaws and Chickasaws, but he did not pay the Creeks. With the Creek regiment in tow, Pike proceeded toward Park Hill to pay Chief John Ross and Treasurer Lewis Ross the funds due the Cherokee Nation by treaty. The 1st Choctaw and Chickasaw Regiment followed slowly behind Pike's lead.[2]

Major General Earl Van Dorn's headquarters were then located in the Boston Mountains just south of Fayetteville in northwestern Arkansas. Van Dorn continued to send out orders for his Confederate units to converge for a major campaign against the Yankee invaders. Pike received orders from Van Dorn to march immediately

2. Duncan, *Reluctant General*, 206–207.

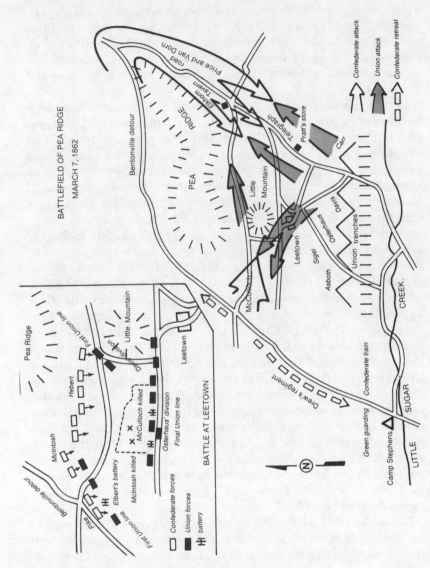

BATTLEFIELD OF PEA RIDGE
MARCH 7, 1862

PEA RIDGE

Bentonville detour

road

Price and Van Dorn

Elkhorn Tavern

Telegraph

Pratt's store

Little Mountain

Carr

McConkith

Leetown

Sigel

Davis

Osterhaus

Asboth

Union trenches

SUGAR

CREEK.

LITTLE

Camp Stephens

Green guarding Confederate train

Drew's regiment

Confederate attack

Union attack

Confederate retreat

Pea Ridge

First Union line

Little Mountain

Davis's division

Leetown

Hebert

McIntosh

Osterhaus division

Final Union line

McCulloch killed

McIntosh killed

Elbert's battery

Pike

First Union line

Bentonville detour

BATTLE AT LEETOWN

Confederate forces

Union forces

battery

N

Map by Bill Henderson

for Arkansas and to send at least two couriers to Van Dorn's headquarters each day to keep him apprised of his progress.[3]

Drew's regiment received orders from General Pike on March 3,
1862, to move along the Cane Hill Road from Evansville to Fayetteville, Arkansas, to join Van Dorn's army. Drew ordered a forced
march. The Cherokee Mounted Rifles were to carry only light equipment, and the regimental baggage train was to travel "at its own
pace" so as not to hinder the troops' progress. The regiment was to
get corn along the road or to haul it with them. Drew had about five
hundred men. The desertions from his regiment the previous December had severely reduced the number of effectives available for
the coming campaign in Arkansas. Similar orders were sent to Colonel Stand Watie's Cherokee regiment and the other units that were
part of General Albert Pike's Indian Brigade.[4]

Many of the Cherokees and other Confederate Indians believed
that Van Dorn's orders betrayed the treaties between their governments and the Confederate States. The Confederate treaty with the
Cherokee Nation, after all, stated that no Indian troops were to be
used outside the Indian nations without each nation's consent.
Some of Drew's Cherokees felt that they had not been asked if they
wanted to go to Arkansas to fight Yankees; they had been ordered
to go.

With the departure of Drew's and Watie's regiments for Arkansas
the only military force left to defend the Cherokee Nation was a
force of only twenty-two Cherokees commanded by Captain Henry
Chambers. This force was recruited on March 3, 1862, to guard the
now fat Cherokee treasury. Pay for the enlisted men in this small
force was one dollar per day, and each of the two captains was to
receive two dollars per day.[5]

On March 1, 1862, as stipulated by the Confederate treaty with
the Cherokees, General Albert Pike had paid the Cherokees $70,000
in gold and $150,000 in Confederate treasury notes procured from
Richmond. This money was a loan or an advance on the expected
price for the Cherokee Neutral Lands, much of which was owned by
Chief Ross and his family. The company guarding the Cherokee
treasury was to be disbanded on the return of the two regiments to

3. *OR*, VIII, 763–64.
4. Brigadier General Dabney H. Maury to Drew, March 4, 1862, in Foreman Papers, Gilcrease Institute; *OR*, VIII, 764–65.
5. Company muster, March 4, 1862, in Foreman Papers, Gilcrease Institute.

their homeland after the Arkansas campaign. The 1st Creek Regiment and two hundred Texas cavalrymen accompanied Pike to Park Hill when the money was paid to the Cherokees. General Pike and his command left Park Hill to collect the other units of the Indian Brigade and head for Arkansas, following Van Dorn's orders.[6]

Chief John Ross accompanied Drew's regiment on its march to Arkansas to a point twelve miles east of Park Hill. Ross hoped to encourage the regiment on its first campaign against armed white troops. Ross originally intended to travel with Drew's regiment into Arkansas, but he decided to return to Park Hill out of fear that members of Watie's regiment might retaliate against him. On his return to Park Hill on February 25, 1862, Chief Ross wrote to General Albert Pike, "In my opinion, this regiment will not fail to do their whole duty, wherever the conflict with the common enemy shall take place."[7]

Drew's mounted column was overtaken about six miles south of Bentonville, Arkansas, at Smith's Mill or Osage Mills, on Thursday, March 6, 1862, by Brigadier General Albert Pike with Watie's regiment and Captain Otis G. Welch's Texas Squadron. The 1st Choctaw and Chickasaw Regiment still followed far behind General Pike and his escort even though it had been paid at Cantonment Davis. The Choctaws and Chickasaws were less than eager to leave the Indian nations to fight in the Confederate state of Arkansas. Without General Pike prodding them along, the Choctaws and Chickasaws dragged their heels.[8]

Pike's column proceeded north with Drew's regiment, and near Bentonville, Arkansas, scouts from the regiment captured seven Union soldiers. The captured Yankees were probably from Brigadier General Franz Sigel's command, which had just been pushed from Bentonville toward Elkhorn Tavern by Van Dorn's advance forces. Sigel was a former minister of a revolutionary German government and an instructor in a St. Louis military school.

When Drew's Cherokee regiment encountered General Sigel's two divisions, the Union soldiers were retreating east to join the main Union army before the concentrating Confederate forces could surround them and cut them off. This retreat was the result of a four-to-five-hour running battle in which General Price's advance guard

6. Abel, *American Indian as Participant*, 138.
7. Thoburn (ed.), "Cherokee Question," 189–90.
8. *OR*, VIII, 287.

had driven the Union force from Bentonville to its trenches on the bluffs overlooking Little Sugar Creek. Once on the bluffs, the Union commander, General Samuel Curtis, a civil engineer, had his army dig earthworks because he expected a frontal assault by Van Dorn's army. Drew's regiment turned the Union prisoners over to the proper Confederate authorities and awaited further orders.[9]

Curtis' army of about 10,500 effective soldiers and forty-nine cannon prepared for the expected attack by Van Dorn's army of about 16,000 men and more than sixty cannon. Although Curtis' force was outnumbered, his troops were more rested because Van Dorn's army had been under forced marches so as to concentrate at Bentonville. The Union force was better armed and had a more centralized command structure, whereas Van Dorn was new to his army and his soldiers were not used to joint operations with large bodies of troops. There was considerable confusion in the Confederate army because of the friction between its commanders. The weather was also very cold, snow having fallen on March 5, the previous day. The subfreezing weather was hard on the Cherokees because most of their wagons and equipment were still far behind them.

Late in the afternoon of March 6, 1862, General Pike's Indian Brigade, which included Drew's regiment, reached Brigadier General Ben McCulloch's division. Pike's brigade camped within two miles of the main Confederate forces at Camp Stephens, which was strategically located at the junction of two roads seven miles northeast of Bentonville on Little Sugar Creek.

At 9:30 P.M. on March 6, 1862, General Pike was told of General Van Dorn's plans for the impending attack that was to take place in the early morning hours of March 7. Instead of a frontal assault on the fortified Union positions on the bluff on Little Sugar Creek, the Confederate army was to make a wide circle to the north around the Union positions and attack the unfortified rear guard in a two-pronged pincer movement, cutting the Union army off from its supply lines to Springfield and Rolla, Missouri. McCulloch's Texas and Arkansas division, along with Pike's Indian Brigade, was to attack from the north through the small village of Leetown and rout the unsuspecting Union troops.[10]

9. *Ibid.*, XIII, 820.
10. *Ibid.*, VIII, 287.

Leetown was named after John W. Lee, a first cousin of Confederate General Robert E. Lee, and consisted of only about six or so houses and some outbuildings. General Sterling Price's Missouri division was to attack down the Telegraph Road through Elkhorn Tavern, an inn and stagecoach stop at the crossing of several key roads. Elkhorn Tavern was on the road where the Butterfield Overland Mail Company ran its stagecoaches from St. Louis, Missouri, to San Francisco, California. In 1860 a telegraph line was strung along the road, and thereafter it was known as the Telegraph Road.

About midnight Drew's regiment marched to its assigned positions with the remainder of Pike's brigade. A member of Price's division in the 1st Missouri Brigade later wrote of the Indians' movements: "They came trotting gaily into camp yelling forth a wild war whoop that startled the army out of all its propriety. Their faces were painted for they were 'on the warpath,' their long black hair qued in clubs hung down their backs, buckskin shirts, leggins, and moccasins adorned with little bells and rattles, together with bright colored turkey feathers fastened on their heads completed unique uniforms not strictly cut according to military regulations. Armed only with tomahawk, and war clubs, and presented an appearance somewhat savage, but they were mostly Cherokees, cool and cautious in danger, active and sinewy in person, fine specimens of 'the noble red man.'"[11]

One Texan later wrote, "En Route to the field of battle, we passed the Indian Brigade of General Pike, all of whom were painted, in conformity to the horrid customs of their people." A Confederate surgeon wrote that on the morning of battle he observed almost three hundred Indians daubing their faces black with charcoal. A chief informed him that "the Indians when going into a fight, painted their faces red; but that when suffering from hunger they color black. They had been without food for two days."[12]

Although the Confederate witnesses may have exaggerated the appearance of the Cherokees, it should be remembered that not all Cherokees were "civilized" or had adopted the white man's way of dress. Many traditional Cherokees clung to the old customs and dressed accordingly. Although many had been educated in religious

11. R. S. Bevier, *History of the First and Second Missouri Confederate Birgades, 1861–1862* (St. Louis, 1879), 92–93.
12. Edwin C. Bearss, "The Indians at Pea Ridge" (typescript, Pea Ridge National Military Park), Notes C. IV, n. 1.

schools, the use of war paint and scalping were traditions hard to suppress.

Pike's Indian Brigade passed McCulloch's baggage train but had to wait until sunrise while McCulloch's infantry in front crossed Little Sugar Creek on a small bridge of rails or poles laid side by side so the infantry would not have to ford the tiny, ice-cold creek. The intense cold and the exhaustion caused by the long marches made the troops unwilling to ford the stream so they awaited their turn to cross the "bridge." The Confederate column was delayed by trees, which had been cut down by advance Union scouts to block the movement of the Confederate horses, wagons, and artillery. Pike's brigade, following at the rear of McCulloch's division, was halted at Pea Vine Ridge, where Pike was instructed to march behind Colonel William B. Sims's 9th Texas Cavalry Regiment down the same road they had just traveled. Evidently someone forgot to tell them to move south to Leetown, and they missed the turnoff. Van Dorn was afraid that Curtis' Union forces might try to cut the Bentonville or Detour Road from Elkhorn Tavern to Bentonville so he ordered McCulloch's division to capture Leetown and prevent any such flanking movement.[13]

After backtracking, Pike's brigade with Drew's Cherokees rode south off the Bentonville Road and headed through the woods. Pike's orders were to march with General McCulloch's division four and one-half miles to the south of the road to attack the Union forces forming at Leetown, some one and one-half miles north of Federal positions along the bluff overlooking Little Sugar Creek. By that time the Confederate flanking movement was several hours behind schedule because of delays and confusion. The first elements got in position at about 10 A.M. The Confederate delays allowed Union scouts to give a warning so the Union forces had time to rush troops to the northwest to meet the Confederate flanking movements. Before Pike's brigade encountered Union positions, fighting had already started around Elkhorn Tavern, within earshot. The Confederates lost their element of surprise, and Major General Van Dorn, who was ill, rode in an ambulance on to the battlefield.[14]

After marching southeast for a mile along a narrow road, Drew's regiment and the Indian Brigade discovered a Union force on the

13. *OR*, VIII, 287.
14. *Ibid.*

prairie about three hundred yards away. These troops were the advance elements of Colonel Peter J. Osterhaus' 1st Division. Osterhaus was born in Prussia, had served in the Prussian army, and later settled in St. Louis. He enlisted as a private in the 12th Missouri Infantry Regiment and quickly was promoted to colonel. This advance Union force consisted of Captain Gustavus M. Elbert's flying battery of three James Rifles in the Missouri Light Artillery, two companies of the 1st Missouri Cavalry Regiment, the Benton Hussars (5th Missouri Cavalry Regiment), and the Fremont Hussars (4th Missouri Cavalry Regiment).[15]

Led by Colonel Cyrus Bussey, the Union force had been ordered to meet the flanking Confederates and delay them until reinforcements could arrive. Colonel Nicholas Greusel and a brigade consisting of the 36th Illinois Infantry Regiment, the 22d Indiana Infantry Regiment, the 12th Missouri Infantry Regiment, six guns of the 4th Battery of Ohio Light Artillery, and three guns of Captain Martin Welfrey's Independent Missouri Battery were also positioned in the fields to the north and west of Leetown to blunt McCulloch's attack.[16]

While Brigadier General James McQueen McIntosh's brigade in McCulloch's division charged the Federals in a large field to their east, Pike drew the 1,000 men of his brigade along with Colonel Sims's 150 to 200 Texans into a line near some woods as the three-gun Union battery commenced shelling the Confederate columns. Colonel Drew's mounted Cherokees were interspersed with Colonel Watie's dismounted Cherokees in the right flank of the Confederate line at a fence facing the Union battery. On the opposite end of the line were Sims's Texans, and in the middle was Welch's Texas Squadron.

With war whoops and Rebel yells, a surging mass of Cherokees and Texans erupted, breaking down the fence in front of them as they charged the Union battery. Part of Colonel Sims's Texas regiment remained at the fence to cover the attack. It was almost noon, and in a matter of seconds the Confederates, armed with a wide assortment of weapons, overwhelmed the Union battery. The Union survivors were sent reeling toward the main body of their army. The Union artillerymen took all of their caissons and all but

15. *Ibid.*
16. Wiley Britton, *The Civil War on the Border, 1861–1862* (New York, 1890), 242–44.

four of their horses and fled, leaving the precious cannons behind, unspiked. It was now noon. Instead of chasing the fleeing Union troops, Pike's Indians stopped to examine their trophies of war, the cannons.[17]

The companies of the 1st Missouri Cavalry Regiment with the battery broke and fled through Leetown, racing through the lines of the advancing 59th Illinois Infantry Regiment that was moving up to reinforce the shattered Union line. Colonel Greusel's brigade continued to advance through the fleeing cavalrymen and artillerymen of Bussey's small force.[18]

Between thirty and forty bluecoats lay dead around the three captured cannons on the field. With two dead and one wounded, Drew's regiment suffered the highest Confederate loss in the charge. The Texans had one dead and one wounded. Although the Cherokees played a significant part in taking the battery, many historians would later ignore their presence in the fight and give credit only to the Texas units for capturing the Union battery. In reality, it was a joint effort.

Many of the Union dead were scalped and mutilated by the Cherokees in the heat of battle during and shortly after the battery's capture, a fact that would later be given widespread publication in northern newspapers. Colonel Cyrus Bussey of the 3d Iowa Cavalry Regiment later returned to the battery site and found twenty-five of his regiment dead around the guns. Eight of the Iowans had been scalped, and several had been pierced through the neck by knives in addition to receiving bullet wounds. The adjutant of the 3d Iowa Cavalry Regiment thought some of his men had been killed after being wounded. The full-bloods in Drew's regiment later blamed the mixed-bloods in Watie's regiment for the atrocities, but in fact the blame probably should have been shared by both Cherokee regiments.[19]

After the capture of the Union cannons chaos reigned at the battery site as the Cherokees rode and ran in confusion around the guns, whooping and yelling victoriously for twenty minutes. Many of the Cherokees were reported to have called the cannons wagon-guns or shooting wagons. During this confusion, two additional Union artillery batteries supported by some Union infantry reg-

17. *OR*, VIII, 217, 288.
18. *Ibid.*, 288.
19. *Ibid.*, 206–207.

iments from Osterhaus' division under Colonel Greusel moved up
and began to fire on the disorganized Cherokees and to shell General James McIntosh's brigade.

Drew's regiment was positioned in a field to the right of the captured battery, but since no one near the battery would listen to his
orders, General Pike was unable to get the cannons turned around
to establish a counterfire against the Union cannons. Captain
Roswell W. Lee of Colonel Cooper's staff also tried to organize the
Indians, but to no avail.[20]

After the Union batteries fired a few artillery shells, the Confederate Cherokees fled back into the cover of the woods from which they
had previously charged. Pike reported that they were in a state of
great trepidation. The Cherokees had not been trained to fight in
open fields in the formal military manner of the day but, rather, to
fight individually in the cover of woods in the frontier fashion. None
of the officers in Drew's regiment had any formal military training.
Drew's men dismounted in the woods, led their horses and ponies
to the rear, and took cover behind the shelter of trees. Watie's men
also took cover behind trees as shells crashed near them.[21]

When several Confederate cavalry regiments near Pike's command advanced toward the Union lines at about 1:30 P.M., Drew led
his regiment across the field to form up near the rear of the 6th Texas
Cavalry Regiment. Pike then ordered Drew to advance with the
Texans when they attacked. The Cherokees were to attack on foot to
"join in the fight in their own fashion." While Drew's regiment
formed in front of the woods, some of Watie's Cherokees finally
wheeled two of the captured cannons into the woods. A Yankee
shell landed nearby, however, and sent the Cherokees of Drew's
regiment fleeing back into the woods for protection.[22]

About 2 P.M. Union Colonel Jefferson C. Davis arrived with part of
his regiments and the 22d Indiana Regiment to strengthen the
Union line. Around 3 P.M. General Pike learned from Major John W.
Whitfield that General Ben McCulloch had been killed while scouting the Union lines and that Brigadier General James McQueen
McIntosh, the second in command of McCulloch's division, had
also been killed in the vicious fighting. McIntosh had become a
brigadier general after his dramatic victory over Opothleyahola in

20. *Ibid.*, 288.
21. Britton, *Civil War on the Border*, 247.
22. *OR*, VIII, 289.

the Cherokee Nation. Another capable Confederate leader, Colonel Louis Hébert of Louisiana, was captured by the Union troops. General Albert Pike became the senior officer in command of the Confederate right wing.[23]

Pike, however, had no knowledge of the roads in the area and very little knowledge of the Confederate battle plan. He had not been in contact with McCulloch or McIntosh during the battle so he did not know the exact position of the Confederate troops. Pike had no formal military training as a commander of a large body of troops. His last command in battle was with an Arkansas company in the Battle of Buena Vista during the Mexican War. He also had no real idea of the strength of the opposing Union forces.

From Round Top, a nearby hill, Pike scouted his portion of the battlefield. He saw part of his forces withdrawing toward the Bentonville–Little Sugar Creek Road, leaving his right flank open to a possible Union attack. He decided to join Van Dorn's main force at Elkhorn Tavern east of Pea Ridge instead of trying to hold his position. Confused and bewildered, Pike gathered what Confederate troops he could find and marched down the road to join the main body of the Confederate army under Van Dorn and Price around Elkhorn Tavern. Before Pike left the Leetown portion of the battlefield, he burned the captured cannons' carriages because he had no caissons with which to haul them off. Several Cherokees were reportedly killed when some gunpowder exploded, but the cannons were left unharmed to be salvaged by the Union troops.[24]

Pike's column had Welch's Texas Squadron in front, followed by the Arkansas and Texas infantry and a Confederate battery. Watie's regiment guarded the column's flanks as it headed north, and the 6th Texas Cavalry Regiment brought up the rear. Although Watie's regiment was with Pike, by some accident Drew's regiment was not informed of the Confederate withdrawal and thus remained behind in the woods without any Confederate support to face the advancing Union forces.[25] Pike sent a courier to inform Drew of the retreat, but for some unknown reason the courier never reached Drew's regiment.[26]

Finding the other Confederate forces in the Leetown area gone

23. *Ibid.*
24. *Ibid.*, 289–90, 301.
25. *Ibid.*, 290.
26. Duncan, *Reluctant General*, 217.

and a large body of Federal forces advancing upon them in the
darkness, Drew's Cherokee regiment beat a hasty retreat south-
westward toward Bentonville and Camp Stephens about two hours
after Pike's retreat. At Camp Stephens Drew's regiment encountered the Confederate baggage and ammunition train guarded by
Brigadier General Martin E. Green and his division of Missouri State
Guard. The train was badly needed by Van Dorn's troops because
their ammunition and supplies had been severely depleted by the
day's fighting.

At Camp Stephens Drew's command also found Colonel B. War-
ren Stone's 6th Texas Cavalry Regiment, which had been part of the
rear guard of Pike's retreating column as it headed toward Elkhorn
Tavern along with the remnants of McCulloch's division to join Van
Dorn and Price. Stone heard that a large force of Union troops was
about to attack the Confederate supply train so Pike ordered him to
ride with his regiment to the train's aid. But there was no Union
attack on the supply train because the Union forces were almost as
disorganized as the Confederates.[27]

Also in Camp Stephens, Drew and his men found two hundred
soldiers from Colonel Daniel N. McIntosh's 1st Creek Regiment as
well as Colonel Douglas H. Cooper's 1st Choctaw and Chickasaw
Regiment, which had finally arrived from Indian Territory. These
two regiments were supposed to have joined Pike's brigade earlier,
but because of dissension within the units about fighting in Arkansas as well as their unhappiness over their pay, they arrived too late
to participate in the first day's battle at Pea Ridge. Most of the men in
these two Indian regiments were still in the Indian nations and had
decided to avoid the big fight with the Union troops in Arkansas.[28]

Colonel Drew and his men remained with the other Confederate
troops at Camp Stephens to protect the wagons and supplies and
thus did not actively participate in the second day of the Battle of Pea
Ridge, or Elkhorn Tavern, on Saturday, March 8, 1862. The Confederate artillery was low on ammunition and could only occasionally
return the fire of the Union artillery, which fired volley after volley
into the Confederate lines. The Confederate officer in charge of
ordnance and supplies could not find the badly needed supply
train. General Green, aware of Van Dorn's desperate need for shells

27. *OR*, VIII, 292.
28. Robert G. Hartje, *Van Dorn: The Life and Times of a Confederate General* (Nashville,
1967), 153.

and gunpowder, was prepared to send the ammunition train to Elkhorn Tavern. Green sent a messenger to Price at Elkhorn Tavern to let him know the train's location and to get orders for the wagon train and its escort. Meanwhile, Colonel Robert C. Wood of Price's staff reached Green with orders to bring up the wagons. Green quickly complied, but the advance group encountered Green's earlier messenger with orders for the wagons to proceed directly to Elm Springs, away from the battle, halfway between Fayetteville and Bentonville. The Confederate forces were losing badly, and Van Dorn's troops had only the supplies they had carried with them the morning of the previous day. The lack of needed supplies and ammunition sealed the Confederates' fate on the second day of battle.[29]

The Confederate wagon train broke camp and proceeded with its escort of Texans and Indians toward Elm Springs, where they camped on the prairie just north of Bentonville on the night of March 8, 1862. The next day the wagon train reached Elm Springs. Drew's regiment, the 1st Creek Regiment, and the 1st Choctaw and Chickasaw Regiment separated from the train and with their own baggage train headed back home to the Indian nations by way of Cincinnati, Arkansas. They felt they had fulfilled their mission for the Confederacy in Arkansas and were more badly needed in the Indian nations.[30]

The main Confederate forces fled southward after being badly mauled during the two-day Battle of Pea Ridge. Union sources reported that Van Dorn's army had lost 1,100 killed, 2,500 wounded, and 1,600 captured or missing. General Van Dorn officially listed his losses at 600 killed or wounded and 200 captured, while the Confederate surgeon general listed the losses as 185 killed, 525 wounded, and 300 captured. Other sources put the Confederate losses at 800 to 1,000 killed and wounded with 200 to 300 captured. General Samuel R. Curtis' Union army listed on its revised report losses of 203 killed, 980 wounded, and 201 captured or missing in the battle.[31]

A few days after the Battle of Pea Ridge, General Pike found Drew's regiment and the other two Indian regiments waiting for him at Cincinnati, Arkansas. Until then Pike had not known what had happened to the rest of his Indian Brigade. Watie's regiment returned to the Cherokee Nation after discovering that the Confed-

29. Ibid., 153–55.
30. OR, VIII, 292.
31. Ibid.; Hartje, Van Dorn, 160.

erate wagon train it was supposed to escort from Elm Springs had already left.[32]

At Pea Ridge Drew's regiment lost four of its number as Union prisoners: Captain Richard Fields of Company F, Surgeon James P. Evans, Hospital Steward Walter N. Evans, who was the surgeon's son, and Private James Piddy. All were taken to the Union prison at Alton, Illinois. Dr. Evans was discharged on parole on June 23, 1862, and his son was discharged on July 11. Captain Richard Fields was exchanged on May 17, 1862, but Private Piddy died of disease on March 30, 1862, while still in prison.[33]

Considering the conditions under which they were fighting, the Cherokee regiments gave a good account of themselves. Chief John Ross was unhappy because Watie's regiment received more recognition from General Pike for its part in the Battle of Pea Ridge than Drew's regiment did. But Pike was outraged because he and his entire Indian Brigade were totally ignored in the Confederate reports owing to his Indians' scalpings at the Union battery.

On March 9, 1862, General Van Dorn asked General Curtis to bury the dead of both sides at Pea Ridge and requested that a Confederate burial party be allowed on the field under a flag of truce, a normal courtesy in the Civil War.[34] Curtis agreed to the truce so the dead on the Pea Ridge battlefield could be attended to by burial parties from both armies. An aide to General Curtis sent a letter to General Van Dorn stating, "The general regrets that we find on the battle-field, contrary to civilized warfare, many of the Federal dead who were tomahawked, scalped, and their bodies shamefully mangled, and expresses a hope that this important struggle may not degenerate to a savage warfare." This letter badly stung the officers in the Confederate high command, many of whom were officers and gentlemen trained in the art of warfare at West Point along with Union officers. Curtis had been one of their former classmates and friends.[35]

General Van Dorn's adjutant responded to Curtis on March 14, 1862, expressing "thanks and gratification on account of the courtesy extended . . . to the burial party sent by him" to the battlefield.

32. Brig. Gen. Samuel R. Curtis, "Composition and Losses of the Union Army," and Major-General Earl Van Dorn, "Composition and Losses of the Confederate Army," in R. V. Johnson and C. C. Buel (eds.), *Battles and Leaders of the Civil War* (4 vols., 1884–88; rpr. New York, 1956), I, 337.
33. *OR*, XIII, 824–26.
34. Duncan, *Reluctant General*, 225–26.
35. *OR*, VIII, 194.

Van Dorn was "pained to learn by" a "letter brought to him by the commanding officer of the party that the remains of some of your [Union] soldiers have been reported . . . to have been scalped, tomahawked, and otherwise mutilated." Van Dorn hoped Curtis had "been misinformed with regard to this matter, the Indians who formed part of his forces having for many years been regarded as civilized people." Van Dorn said he would "unite with" Curtis "in repressing the horrors of this unnatural war" and would cooperate with him. Van Dorn wrote, "Many of our men who surrendered themselves prisoners of war were reported to him as having been murdered in cold blood by their captors, who were alleged to be Germans." Van Dorn asked Curtis to help "in preventing such atrocities in the future, and that the perpetrators of them will be brought to justice, whether German or Choctaw."[36]

The Union government wanted details about the brutality and scalpings in the battle. On April 2, 1862, Chairman Benjamin F. Wade of the Committee on the Conduct of the Present War asked for specific evidence. On May 21, 1862, General Curtis replied, "I have the honor to now lay before the committee the statements and affidavits inclosed, from which it will appear that large forces of Indian savages were engaged against this army at the Battle of Pea Ridge, and that the warfare was conducted by said savages with all the barbarity their merciless and cowardly natures are capable of."[37]

A Northern pamphlet added fuel to the charges against the Indians at Pea Ridge by stating that before the battle General Pike had gathered his Indians and "maddened them with liquor to fire their savage natures, and, with gaudy dress and a large plume on his head, disregarding all the usages of civilized warfare, led them in a carnage of savagery, scalping wounded and helpless soldiers, and committing other atrocities too horrible to mention." The Chicago *Tribune* embellished the story, increasing the number of scalped Union soldiers to one hundred and saying, "Col. Albert Pike . . . deserves and will undoubtedly receive eternal infamy." The New York *Tribune* called Pike "a ferocious fish." Pike's hometown newspaper, the Boston *Evening Transcript*, on March 15, 1862, said, "The meanest, the most rascally, the most malevolent of the rebels who are at war with the United States Government, are said to be recreant Yankees. Albert Pike is one of these." The paper continued:

36. *Ibid.*, 195.
37. *Ibid.*, 206.

"Renegades are always loathsome creatures, and it is not to be presumed that a more venemous reptile than Albert Pike ever crawled on the face of the earth."[38]

The Indians had acted as might have been expected in a major pitched battle in a white man's war. General Pike examined his surgeons' and assistant surgeons' field hospital reports for information on scalpings of the Union dead. According to Pike, these reports showed that the surgeons found that at least one of the Federal dead was indeed scalped. Pike denounced the scalpings, sending an order to Curtis asserting that they were done by Indians in General McCulloch's command, not his, and that they occurred in a section of the field not held by the Indian troops under his command. Several participants in the battle on the Union side, Captain Samuel P. Curtis, and Corporal George W. Herr said that Texans, not Indians, had mutilated the Union dead.[39]

Northern newspapers had a field day when word of the scalpings reached them. The Civil War was now put into the context of good against evil, of a civilized Union government against a bloodthirsty Confederate government that used savages who scalped white men.

38. Duncan, *Reluctant General*, 228–29.
39. Bearss, "Indians at Pea Ridge," 164.

8
Furlough

Following their defeat at the Battle of Pea Ridge, the weary and worn Cherokees returned to the Cherokee Nation. It was now only a matter of time before the victorious Union forces would invade Cherokee soil. To regroup from the battle, the Confederate Indian Brigade camped at Dwight Mission in the Cherokee Nation. Dwight Mission was established in 1829 by the Presbyterians and was a key center of Indian education and religion. On March 15, 1862, General Pike issued an order expressing horror at seeing a member of his command shoot a wounded Union soldier who was begging for mercy. Pike stated, "The commanding general has also learned with the utmost pain and regret that one, at least, of the enemy's dead was found scalped upon the field. That practice excites horror, leads to cruel retaliation, and would expose the Confederate States to the just reprehension of all civilized nations. . . . Against forces that do not practice it, it is peremptorily forbidden during the present war."[1]

Drew's men were ordered to leave Dwight Mission on March 17, as the Confederate Indian Brigade separated and split up throughout the Indian nations. The sick and about twenty wounded members of Drew's regiment remained at Dwight Mission to recover in the care of missionaries.[2] Four of the wounded later died and were buried in the mission cemetery.[3]

Colonel John Drew removed his men to a camp near the mouth of the Illinois River not far from his home at Webbers Falls. While they were in camp General Pike paid the enlisted men in Drew's regiment the only money many would receive from the Confederacy: twenty-five dollars in cash and a six-month clothing allowance.[4]

Special orders were issued on March 22, 1862, from Cantonment

1. Dean Trickett, "The Civil War in Indian Territory, 1862," *Chronicles of Oklahoma*, XIX (December, 1941), 396.
2. Cooper to Drew, March 17, 1862, in Foreman Papers, Gilcrease Institute.
3. Edward F. Heard, "Dwight Mission Under the American Board" (Master's thesis, University of Tulsa, 1958), 80.
4. Abel, *American Indian as Participant*, 138.

Davis for the Indian regiments to furlough some of their number to give them time to rest and to plant their corn crops. It was vital to the Indians that crops be planted in the spring or there might not be enough food to feed the Indian families and Confederate forces in the Indian nations during the coming winter. John Drew's Cherokee Mounted Rifles were to furlough as many men as was "necessary, not exceeding two thirds." If, by chance, Union troops invaded the Indian nations, the furloughed men were to rejoin their regiment immediately to repel the invaders.[5]

On March 22, part of Drew's regiment was ordered to proceed to Webbers Falls to guard a large quantity of Confederate commissary and ordnance stores gathered there. Colonel Douglas H. Cooper wanted at least half if not all of Drew's regiment on the west side of the Arkansas River near Webbers Falls. A thirty-day ration of flour and salt meats from Cantonment Davis was set aside for the regiment to supply its short-term needs. Since no transport was available at the post to move the food to his regiment, Drew had to send his own regimental wagons to get the supplies.[6]

Chief John Ross, however, was uneasy about his regiment being isolated in the southwest corner of his nation away from the Cherokee capital of Tahlequah. The old chief wanted his regiment near the seat of his government in case of trouble, whether military or factional. The Cherokee treasury and records were unprotected; only Stand Watie's forces were in the area. Therefore, Chief Ross asked that some troops from Drew's regiment be stationed near his home at Park Hill. On the question of food supplies for the regiment, Ross said he had "no doubt that forage can be procured for Colonel Drew's men in this vicinity by hauling it in from the farms of the surrounding districts." In answer to the old chief's appeal, part of Drew's regiment was sent to Park Hill.[7] Ross was feeling particularly vulnerable because most of the Confederate forces under Brigadier General Albert Pike were now in the southern reaches of the Indian nations near the Red River. Before leaving on furlough, the soldiers in Drew's regiment were told that the Confederate government would not pay them in the near future.[8]

After the Union victory at Pea Ridge the flow of Confederate

5. Special Orders, March 22, 1862, in Foreman Papers, Gilcrease Institute.
6. Carroll to Drew, March 22, 1862, *ibid*.
7. Abel, *American Indian as Participant*, 111.
8. Drew to Queensbury, March 25, 1862, in Foreman Papers, Gilcrease Institute.

supplies was concentrated in areas east of the Mississippi River rather than the Trans-Mississippi District. General Earl Van Dorn and most of his army were ordered east across the Mississippi River to Corinth, Mississippi, to join General Albert Sidney Johnston's army. The Indian regiments were left to fend for themselves in the Indian nations. Supplies at Fort Smith bound for General Pike's Indian Brigade, which included Drew's regiment, were confiscated by Van Dorn's troops before they left for Mississippi. Boxes of clothes, shoes, gunpowder, munitions, and all the tents bound for Indian units in Indian Territory were instead given to white Confederate units, many of which had abandoned their equipment during their chaotic retreat from the Battle of Pea Ridge.[9]

Brigadier General Albert Pike withdrew his command from Cantonment Davis to Fort McCulloch on the Blue River in the Choctaw Nation just north of the Texas line. Pike constructed extensive earthworks at Fort McCulloch to defend against any possible Union invasion. This new post was established more for the defense of Texas than of the Indian nations. For all practical purposes, only Drew's and Watie's partially furloughed regiments were left to defend the Cherokee Nation, the southern buffer to the Union state of Kansas.

A letter from Pike to Watie ordered Drew's and Watie's regiments to give Pike "notice of the approach of the enemy, harass his flanks and rear, stampede his animals, destroy his small foraging parties, and at last if he still advances, gaining his front, join me within my lines and aid in utterly defeating him there." When Van Dorn's command pulled out of western Arkansas, abandoning Fort Smith in mid-April, the Cherokees were indeed alone.[10]

By the middle of April, 1862, Major Pegg placed some soldiers in camp at Park Hill to guard the Cherokee chief and government. Twenty men of Drew's regiment from Captain John Porum Davis' company were sent from Webbers Falls to guard Cantonment Davis and its supplies, which Pike had abandoned in his haste to flee south to set up Fort McCulloch. The men of Drew's regiment were now widely dispersed in camps and homes throughout the Cherokee Nation.[11]

Watie's regiment, stationed on the northern border of the Cher-

9. *OR*, XIII, 820–23, 846–47, 860–64, 938–40.
10. Edward Everett Dale, "The Cherokees in the Confederacy," *Journal of Southern History*, XIII (May, 1947), 169.
11. Dale and Litton (eds.), *Cherokee Cavaliers*, 116.

okee Nation, was ordered to make raids into Kansas and Missouri to harass the Union troops there. On April 26, 1862, Watie's regiment with Colonel John T. Coffee's Missourians fought a skirmish at Neosho, Missouri, against the Union 1st Missouri Cavalry Regiment. In this battle Watie's regiment suffered two killed and five wounded while other Confederate losses brought the total to thirty killed and wounded with sixty-two taken prisoner. The Union forces lost thirty-one killed and several wounded with three captured. This fight was a preview of future Union activity along the Cherokee border.[12]

On April 30, 1862, the Cherokee National Council, referring to the scalpings and atrocities at the Battle of Pea Ridge, passed a resolution that the war be fought with the "most humane principles which govern the usages of war among civilized nations" and "recommend[ed] to the troops of this nation . . . to avoid any acts toward captured or fallen foes that would be incompatible with such usages." The Indians were to stop taking scalps. On May 26, 1862, General P. G. T. Beauregard, commander of the Western Department of the Confederacy, appointed Arkansas politician Major General Thomas Carmichael Hindman as commander of the Trans-Mississippi District, replacing Earl Van Dorn. Hindman took over a Confederate district hard-pressed by Union forces on all fronts.[13]

Sometime in May of 1862, Lieutenant Colonel William P. Ross visited General Albert Pike at his camp at Fort McCulloch and informed him that his appointment as a brigadier general would please his uncle, Chief John Ross, immensely. General Pike wrote the Confederate War Department on the subject but received no reply. Promoting an officer of a regiment that had in part deserted to the Union side to the position of general probably did not seem rational to the Confederate high command, especially in light of the publicity given to the scalpings at the Battle of Pea Ridge.[14]

Furthermore, if Colonel John Drew or Lieutenant Colonel William P. Ross had been given a commission as general it would have given Chief Ross a means of directly controlling Colonel Stand Watie's regiment. Once again Chief Ross was trying to control Stand Watie and his followers, and once again Ross's political ploy failed.

12. Pegg to Drew, April 14, 1862, in Foreman Papers, Gilcrease Institute.
13. *OR*, XIII, 826, 828–29.
14. Abel, *American Indian as Participant*, 139.

On May 31, 1862, Confederate Missouri troops under Colonel John T. Coffee, assisted by Watie's regiment, badly mauled a Union scouting party of five hundred men of the 14th Missouri Cavalry Regiment and the 10th Illinois Cavalry Regiment in another battle at Neosho, Missouri. The victorious Confederates captured some Union supplies. Union casualties were two killed, eight wounded, and one captured, while the Confederates counted at least one killed. Watie and his men then withdrew to their home camp on Cowskin Prairie in the Cherokee Nation.[15]

Colonel Douglas H. Cooper, at his headquarters at Skulleyville, feared that a possible Federal advance was indicated by the increased Union activity on the northern border of the Cherokee Nation and ordered the two Cherokee regiments to muster what men they could and take a position on the Telegraph Road between Evansville and Maysville, Arkansas. The Cherokees were ordered to invade Union-held territory in southwestern Missouri using all but two to four companies of Drew's regiment, which were to guard the "Funds, Archives, and authorities of the Cherokee Nation" at Park Hill.[16]

In Kansas, meanwhile, Colonel Charles Doubleday was organizing a Union expedition to cut off and destroy Watie's troops and to march on Confederate-held Fort Gibson in the Cherokee Nation. Colonel Doubleday assembled a force on June 1, 1862, at Shoal Creek and marched down the Spring River toward Watie's camp on Cowskin Prairie.

Before Cooper's orders to invade Kansas could be carried out by Watie and Drew, a force of a thousand Union soldiers of the 2d Ohio Cavalry Regiment and several cannons under the command of Colonel Charles Doubleday reached the Grand River about dark on the evening of June 6, 1862. Stand Watie's Confederate camp was only about three miles away. Watie had about four hundred men in the camp at his sawmill on Cowskin Prairie and did not expect the rest of his regiment to join him for a few days because they were still on furlough. Under cover of artillery, the Union force attacked, and Watie's good friend and aide Lieutenant Colonel William Penn Adair was killed. Watie's regiment scattered into the night and left its

15. *OR*, XIII, 90–95.
16. Cooper to Drew, May 6, 1862, in Foreman Papers, Gilcrease Institute.

supplies and some five to six hundred head of cattle and horses to the Union forces.[17]

Thinking the skirmish at Cowskin Prairie was the beginning of the expected Union invasion, Lieutenant Colonel William P. Ross, commanding Drew's regiment's guard at Park Hill, sent out scouts to locate any nearby Union forces. He asked Drew for more ammunition and ordered the rest of Drew's regiment to assemble forthwith. The skirmish at Cowskin Prairie was no invasion, however. It was one of a series of scouting expeditions. The Union forces in Kansas were still disorganized and in training.[18]

Colonel Doubleday was soon replaced at Brigadier General James G. Blunt's orders, and Colonel William Weer became commander of the Indian expedition encamped on the border of Kansas and the Cherokee Nation. Weer was the commander of the 10th Kansas Infantry Regiment and was known as an able lawyer from Wyandotte, Kansas. Weer, however, had a bad drinking habit that sometimes made him unfit for command. Lieutenant Colonel James G. Blunt was appointed brigadier general of Kansas volunteers in April, 1862, because of his political connections and was assigned to command the Union Department of Kansas, which included Indian Territory. Blunt was a Kansas physician and lawyer and was a strong abolitionist as well as a political ally of radical Kansas Senator James H. Lane. With Blunt assigned to headquarters at Fort Leavenworth, Weer, as the senior colonel at Baxter Springs, Kansas, became commander of the Indian expedition assembling on the Cherokee Nation's border. Weer waited on the Kansas border for additional Union reinforcements while he organized and armed the 1st and 2d Kansas Indian Home Guard regiments. These two regiments were composed of refugees from Indian Territory, many of whom were survivors of Opothleyahola's army.[19]

With the coming of summer in the Cherokee Nation, the Confederate Indian regiments were still serving without pay or the promised arms, ammunition, clothing, and commissary supplies. In the eyes of many of the Cherokees, the Confederacy had broken its treaty with them. Some of the Cherokees serving in the Confederate

17. *OR*, XIII, 102; Watie to Drew, May 9, 1862, in Foreman Papers, Gilcrease Institute.

18. W. P. Ross to Drew, May 10, 1862, in Foreman Papers, Gilcrease Institute.

19. Edwin C. McReynolds, *Missouri: A History of the Crossroads State* (Norman, 1975), 246.

army still had not even been officially mustered into that army. The Cherokees were still undisciplined, armed mostly with only squirrel rifles and shotguns, and many were mounted on ponies. Many Indians could not speak or write English and understood little about the Confederacy. The Indians were also still afraid of being sent east across the Mississippi River without their consent and contrary to their treaties because most of the Texas units that had earlier served in the Cherokee Nation were now fighting in the East.[20]

From his headquarters just over the border from the Cherokee Nation in Kansas, Colonel William Weer asked for more arms and supplies from the Union high command. Weer was concerned about Confederate guerrillas in Missouri as well as regular Confederate troops in the Indian nations. Colonel Weer sent Indian runners into the Indian nations to notify the pro-Union Indians to prepare for the coming Union invasion.[21]

While on patrol in June, 1862, Union Osage scouts from Kansas encountered some pro-Union Cherokees on their way to join the Union camps in Kansas. On June 13, 1862, Weer reported that these Cherokee messengers brought word of "a secret society of Union Indians called Ke-too-wah" composed of some two thousand warriors led by an Indian called Salmon. Salmon wanted Colonel Weer to notify him secretly of any coming Union invasion, and he begged not to be abandoned by the Union because the Confederate Indians were persecuting the pro-Union Indians still in the Indian nations. The recent defeat of Watie's command by Doubleday brought an increasing fear among the loyal Indians of reprisal by Watie's men. On June 13, 1862, Colonel Weer wrote that Chief "John Ross is undoubtedly with us, and will come out openly when we reach there."[22]

As the Union forces gathered to invade the Cherokee Nation, parties of pro-Union Indians arrived daily in Kansas to join the newly mustered Kansas Indian Home Guard regiments. The 1st Kansas Indian Home Guard Regiment was composed of eight companies of Creeks and two companies of Seminoles; the 2d Kansas Indian Home Guard Regiment consisted of Creeks, Cherokees, Choctaws, Chickasaws, and Osages. Both regiments were staffed

20. *OR*, XIII, 937–38.
21. Wiley Britton, *The Union Indian Brigade in the Civil War* (Kansas City, 1922), 62–63.
22. *OR*, XIII, 430–31.

only by white Kansas officers, generally from white regiments, when organized. These Indian regiments contained many of the same Union Indians who had survived the defeat of Opothleya-hola's band in December, 1861.[23]

On June 23, 1862, Colonel Douglas H. Cooper was given command of most of the Confederate units north of the Canadian River in Indian Territory, allowing him to act independently of Brigadier General Albert Pike. Cooper was directed not to use Indian troops outside of the Indian nations without their consent, and the Indians were ordered not to make unauthorized raids into Union territory for booty or revenge.

On June 26, 1862, Lieutenant James Phillips, acting assistant adjutant general of the Indian expedition for Colonel Weer at Baxter Springs, Kansas, wrote Chief John Ross warning him of the impending Union invasion: "I have learned from your friends with me that you and your people are truly loyal to the Government of the United States; but from stress of circumstances have not been able to carry out your loyal principles during the present unholy rebellion." Lieutenant Phillips, speaking for Colonel Weer, said, "My purpose is to afford you protection and to relieve you and your Country from your present embarrassment and to give you and all your friends an opportunity to show their loyalty to the United States Government."[24]

Colonel William Weer now had in his Indian expedition some six thousand men, consisting of Colonel William F. Cloud's 2d Kansas Cavalry Regiment, Colonel William R. Judson's 6th Kansas Cavalry Regiment, Colonel Edward Lynde's 9th Kansas Cavalry Regiment, Colonel William Weer's 10th Kansas Infantry Regiment, Colonel Frederick Salomon's 9th Wisconsin Infantry Regiment, Colonel Charles Doubleday's 2d Ohio Cavalry Regiment, Colonel Robert W. Furnas' 1st Kansas Indian Home Guard Regiment, Colonel John Ritchie's 2d Kansas Indian Home Guard Regiment, Captain Allen's 1st Kansas Battery, and Captain David G. Rabb's 2d Indiana Battery.[25]

Federal Indian Superintendent William G. Coffin sent two special Indian agents, E. H. Carruth and H. W. Martin, to accompany the

23. *Ibid.*, 443–44.
24. *Ibid.*, 450.
25. James G. Blunt, "General Blunt's Account of His Civil War Experience," *Kansas Historical Quarterly*, I (May, 1932), 223.

Federal expedition to provide aid to the refugee loyal Indians in the return to their homeland. These Indian agents were to aid in the Indian resettlement and to coordinate with the army on Indian matters.[26]

The 2d Kansas Indian Home Guard Regiment contained many Cherokees, including a number of recent deserters from Drew's regiment. Among its officers were Captain James McDaniel, who commanded Company A, and the Reverend John B. Jones, who served as the regiment's chaplain. The Indian refugees were eager to return to their homeland and inflict retribution on their red brothers and sisters who had followed the Confederate flag and had burned and pillaged the pro-Union Indians' homes. These refugee Indian families gathered around the Union army camps west of Baxter Springs, Kansas, in anticipation of the Union invasion of the Indian nations and their return home.

By June 26, 1862, the appeals for reinforcements by Chief John Ross, Colonel Stand Watie, and Colonel John Drew to General Thomas C. Hindman resulted in Colonel J. J. Clarkson of Missouri being put in command of the white troops in the Cherokee Nation. Colonel Clarkson brought a newly formed battalion of one hundred white troops into the Cherokee Nation to reinforce the two Cherokee regiments already there. This small Confederate force was ill prepared to face the Union forces gathering at Fort Scott and Baxter Springs in Kansas and at Neosho, Missouri. Clarkson had ambitious plans to raid the Santa Fe Trail or Union towns in Kansas.[27]

On June 28, 1862, the Union Indian expedition at last moved into the Cherokee Nation with one brigade going down the west side of the Grand River from Baxter Springs, Kansas, while the other marched from Neosho, Missouri. Colonel Weer received information that Brigadier General James S. Raines, Colonel Watie, and Colonel Coffee had Confederate troops camped in and around Cowskin Prairie so he proceeded with caution. Weer's force crossed over to the east side of the Grand River at Hudson's Crossing (Carey's Ferry) and camped on Cowskin Prairie on June 29. At Round Grove in the Cowskin Prairie about three miles from the ford on the Grand River a small skirmish with a mounted force of some 150 Confederates resulted in the capture of 3 Confederate pickets, 12 other pris-

26. Wardell, *Political History,* 152.
27. *OR,* XIII, 858.

oners, and some livestock. The Confederate force under Colonel Watie retreated without putting up much fight. Colonel Weer reported of the Cherokees, "I have information from the south sufficient to satisfy me that the whole tribe can be induced to surrender." An easy Union occupation of the Cherokee Nation appeared likely. Following closely behind the invading Union cavalry columns were some 1,500 Indian refugee women and children who had spent the winter in Kansas.[28]

Union cavalry from the 6th Kansas Cavalry Regiment with some Cherokee scouts under Lieutenant Colonel Lewis R. Jewell were sent to scout between the Grand River and Maysville, Arkansas. The Confederate Cherokee families began to flee from the Cherokee Nation into the Creek, Choctaw, and Chickasaw nations, Arkansas, and Texas to escape reprisals by the invading Union Cherokees. The tables had been turned, and now it was the Confederate Indians' turn to become victims and refugees. Information from Cherokees encountered by Jewell's scouting party indicated that the camp of the white Confederate troops under Colonel J. J. Clarkson was located near Locust Grove and that Colonel Watie had another force in camp on Spavinaw Creek near some of his sawmills.

Colonel Weer boldly decided to strike the Confederate camps of both Colonel Watie and Colonel Clarkson before additional Confederate forces could rush into the Cherokee Nation and set up a more formidable defense. Weer sent his baggage and supply trains, some artillery, the 2d Ohio Cavalry, the 9th Wisconsin Infantry, and the 12th Wisconsin Infantry under Colonel Salomon from Round Grove to the west side of the Grand River, where they marched down the Fort Scott–Fort Gibson Military Road to camp at Cabin Creek.[29]

Colonel Weer took a battalion of the 10th Kansas Infantry Regiment in wagons under Captain Mathew Quigg, a battalion of the 9th Kansas Cavalry Regiment under Major Edwin P. Bancroft, part of the 1st Indian Home Guard Regiment, and a section of Captain Rabb's 2d Indiana Battery in a night march down the east side of the Grand River to surprise the Confederate camp at Locust Grove. At the same time, Colonel Weer sent Lieutenant Colonel Jewell with part of his 6th Kansas Cavalry Regiment to march south in a line parallel to and several miles to the east of Colonel Weer's line of

28. *Ibid.*, 458–61.
29. Britton, *Civil War on the Border*, 300–301.

march. Jewell's force was to attack Watie's camp and then join with Weer's force near Grand Saline to complete the sweep through the northern line of Confederate camps.[30] The stage was now set for a bold Union strike into the heart of the Cherokee Nation.

30. Britton, *Union Indian Brigade*, 64–65; Britton, *Civil War on the Border*, 300–301.

9
Disaster

Colonel J. J. Clarkson's Confederate camp was located about two miles east of the Grand River at Locust Grove, a small settlement in the heart of the Cherokee Nation with a post office. Early on the morning of July 3, 1862, as Colonel Clarkson completed his first week as the Confederate military commander of the Cherokee Nation, detachments of the 1st Kansas Indian Home Guard Regiment under Lieutenant Colonel Stephen H. Wattles, the 9th Kansas Cavalry Regiment under Major Edwin P. Bancroft, the 10th Kansas Infantry Regiment in wagons under Captain Mathew Quigg, and Captain Allen's 1st Kansas Battery under Lieutenant Moses D. Baldwin and Lieutenant Taylor of Weer's Union invasion force rushed the poorly picketed and unfortified Confederate camp. The Confederate camp was positioned on a steep, rocky hill with only a narrow road coming up the south side and dense woods on two sides of the hill. The Union force totaled only about two to three hundred men, but they had excellent Indian guides, and Colonel Weer timed his march to arrive at the Confederate camp for the attack at dawn.[1]

The battle raged through the surrounding woods and brush. The Confederates were taken completely by surprise and were in great disorder. Union forces surrounded the camp and pursued the scattering Confederates all day through the forests and hills. Some of the survivors of Clarkson's command headed straight for Fort Smith, Askansas, "without arms and many minus their hats." When it was over, Colonel Clarkson and 110 of his men were Union prisoners, and about 100 Confederates were killed or wounded (some sources give the losses as 40 killed and 25 wounded). The Union force had 2 privates and 1 assistant surgeon killed and 6 wounded. Doctor A. S. Halleday, the assistant surgeon of the 1st Kansas Indian Home Guard Regiment, was accidentally killed by a Union soldier in the 9th Kansas Cavalry Regiment during the fight.

1. Britton, *Union Indian Brigade*, 65.

Only detachments from the 1st Indian Home Guard Regiment and the 9th Kansas Cavalry Regiment took an active part in the battle.[2]

The Federals also captured sixty-four mule teams in the Confederate baggage and supply trains, along with eighty wagons with supplies including salt, flour, and more than fifty kegs of badly needed gunpowder recently arrived from Fort Smith. A large portion of these stores was originally intended for the Confederate Indian regiments but had been waylaid by Clarkson's white command.[3]

East of Locust Grove the column of the 6th Kansas Cavalry Regiment under Lieutenant Colonel Lewis R. Jewell encountered Watie's Cherokee regiment at Watie's mills on Spavinaw Creek. The 6th Kansas Cavalry Regiment followed Watie's detachment after being informed by an Indian family that Watie and three to four hundred of his men had passed by only an hour or so before. Jewell's column rode hard and two hours later sighted Watie's force at an Indian house where Watie had stopped for supper. Watie's guard on the road barely warned Watie in time for him to escape with the Federal cavalry on his heels. Watie's forces did not try to fight but instead broke into small groups and scattered through the brush and hills. Only darkness halted the chase by the tired Union cavalry.[4]

In the running skirmish with Watie's forces the Federals had one casualty and the Confederate Indians lost one killed.[5] Jewell's force totally dispersed Watie's regiment. The Union troops halted only long enough to feed and rest their horses and themselves before marching all night to Locust Grove, where Weer had just destroyed Clarkson's command.[6]

Some of the Confederate survivors of the Battle of Locust Grove entered Tahlequah and Park Hill with tales of the overwhelming might of the Union forces. Immediately the two companies of Drew's regiment stationed in both of the main Cherokee towns panicked. Faced by overwhelmingly superior Union forces, which included members of some of their own families, and with little hope of Confederate reinforcements, the Confederate Cherokees of

2. *OR*, XIII, 137, 963–65.
3. Britton, *Civil War on the Border*, 302–303.
4. *Ibid.*, 301–302.
5. *OR*, XIII, 138.
6. Britton, *Union Indian Brigade*, 65.

the Ross party wavered in their support of the Stars and Bars. Colonel Weer's and Lieutenant Colonel Jewell's united force rested one day at Locust Grove and then marched to Grand Saline with their Confederate prisoners and the captured wagons loaded with supplies. At Grand Saline they destroyed the Cherokee salt works that supplied Indian Territory and western Arkansas with salt from salt springs. They crossed the Grand River and joined the rest of the Union expedition, which had set up camp at Cabin Creek on the Texas Road or the Fort Scott–Fort Gibson Military Road.[7]

To celebrate Independence Day and their victory at Locust Grove the Union invasion forces at Cabin Creek divided their Confederate booty. Much of the captured clothing went to the refugee Indians traveling with the expedition. The Indians who had enlisted in the Union Army sent messages to many of their friends who were still in the Confederate army or had not enlisted in any army requesting that they join the Union forces. As a result of the Union victories in the Cherokee Nation, new recruits flocked into the Union camp at Cabin Creek and quickly brought Colonel John Ritchie's 2d Kansas Indian Home Guard Regiment up to its full allotted strength. Many of these new Union recruits were deserters from Drew's regiment. Several days later, a Union supply train arrived from Kansas with additional supplies for the growing Union expedition.[8]

To gather more recruits, Colonel Ritchie marched his command twenty miles south of Grand Saline to Flat Rock Creek to be deeper in the Cherokee Nation. By the morning of July 6, 1862, more than six hundred Cherokees from John Drew's Regiment of Cherokee Mounted Rifles had joined Ritchie's Union forces. At this point, for all practical purposes, the Confederate unit known as Drew's regiment was disbanded. A group of two hundred Cherokees led by the chaplain of Drew's regiment, the Reverend Lewis Downing, had also joined Ritchie's forces.[9]

Many Negro slaves also migrated to the Union camps to escape their Indian masters. The Kansas regiments contained many abolitionists, who gave shelter and protection to these runaway slaves, called contrabands. Fear of a violent slave revolt was rampant among the Indian slaveowners in the Cherokee Nation as well as among the other tribes in the Indian nations. With almost all of the

7. Britton, *Civil War on the Border*, 303.
8. *Ibid*.
9. *OR*, XIII, 138.

adult males away in the army, the only persons left on the farms to raise crops and cattle were the Indian women and children and their slaves. The loss of the slaves meant a loss of crops and livestock in the future because there would not be enough laborers to run the farms and ranches with the men away at war. Many of these contrabands later joined the Union army.

From his camp on Wolf Creek, Colonel Weer wrote Chief John Ross on July 7, 1862, to try again to determine Chief Ross's position toward the United States now that many members of the Ross party had changed loyalties. Colonel Weer requested a council with Chief Ross to discuss the deteriorating situation in the Cherokee Nation. Weer's message was carried by Dr. Rufus Gilpatrick, Chief Ross's physician, who was now in the Union army. Two young women accompanied Dr. Gilpatrick on the visit to Chief Ross.[10]

Chief Ross refused a council with Colonel Weer and in a July 8, 1862, letter, which was probably carried back by Dr. Gilpatrick, he wrote, "There is no nation of Indians, I venture to say, that has ever been more scrupulous in the faithful observance of their treaty obligations than the Cherokees." Once again the old chief was trying to play the foxy diplomat and gain delay. On July 8 about three hundred Cherokees and thirty Negroes traveled through Park Hill waving a white flag on their way to join Weer's Union force.[11] In the midst of this disaster for the Confederate Cherokees, Lieutenant Colonel William P. Ross returned to Park Hill from a trip to the White River and Little Rock, Arkansas. On July 12, 1862, from Park Hill he wrote to Colonel Drew, who was then stationed at Cantonment Davis, "I greatly regret the Confusion which exists, and owing to the apprehensions entertained of further Negro difficulties, will remain here till I hear from you." Ross added, somewhat hopefully, that he had heard that Major Pegg's command was increasing in size.[12]

Colonel Weer moved the rest of his force to the camp on Flat Rock Creek, where Colonel Weer wrote his commander, Brigadier General James G. Blunt, proposing that the Confederate Cherokees be allowed to return home with the Union army to protect them against retaliation by the Union Indians. Colonel Weer also proposed that a proclamation be issued inviting the Cherokees to abolish slavery by

10. *Ibid.*, 486.
11. *Ibid.*, 464, 486–87.
12. W. P. Ross to Drew, July 12, 1862, in Drew Papers, 62-56.

vote and accept compensation from the United States government for the freed slaves.

Such confusion reigned in the Cherokee Nation in July, 1862, that few people knew what was actually happening or where the Yankee and Confederate forces were. On July 12 Captain Israel G. Vore, assistant quartermaster in Drew's regiment, wrote Colonel Drew offering to send three Missouri teamsters to Major M. W. Buster of Colonel Clarkson's command. He thought they might be good soldiers because they were not good teamsters, and they needed an "escort." Evidently, there was still some thought of trying to reorganize Clarkson's shattered battalion and return it to service.[13]

The pro-Union Cherokees in the Cherokee Nation extracted their revenge on the Confederate Cherokees, burning many of their homes and killing several of them. Confederate Cherokee women and children were forced to flee to the safety of Confederate camps.[14]

Some members of Drew's regiment enlisted in other Confederate companies forming in July, 1862, before their one-year enlistment in Drew's regiment was over. One of these companies later became Company I of the 2d Cherokee Regiment and included Captain John Porum Davis and Lieutenant Charles Drew of Company C of Drew's regiment.

Captain Isaac N. Hildebrand, an officer in Drew's regiment from the Delaware District, wrote Lieutenant Colonel Ross on July 12 that "northern troops have been in this neighborhood and striped [sic] all citizens of their property." Captain Hildebrand believed the Union forces were on the Neosho (Grand) River and that Lieutenant Colonel Ross was on Cabin Creek on his way to the Delaware District with Drew's regiment. This, however, was far from the truth, for Ross and a few of the regiment's officers were still at Park Hill. Captain Hildebrand, who had lost a few head of his cattle to the Union troops, stated that if the Confederate forces were not coming into the Delaware District, he would "be compelled to move south my stock before" he could join Drew's regiment. He was more worried about his livestock than about defending the Cherokee Nation from the invading Union troops.[15]

The Union forces under Colonel William Weer were encamped twelve miles above Fort Gibson on the Grand River in an area that

13. Vore to Drew, July 12, 1862, *ibid.*, 62-55.
14. *OR*, XIII, 138.
15. Hildebrand to W. P. Ross, July 13, 1862, in Drew Papers, 62-59.

was suffering severe drought. The Confederates burned the prairie grass all around his camp, hoping the fires would spread and burn the Union camp. In the hot July sun the Union soldiers successfully combated these fires and saved their camp and supplies. By July 12, 1862, some fifteen hundred new Cherokee recruits joined the Union invasion force. The 2d Kansas Indian Home Guard Regiment was sent to Baxter Springs, Kansas, to protect wagon trains from Confederate raiding parties, to escort captured Confederate soldiers to prison, and to muster in the new soldiers in their regiment. The 3d Kansas Indian Home Guard Regiment was set up to absorb the new Cherokee recruits, which were not put in the 2d Kansas Indian Home Guard Regiment.[16]

On July 12, 1862, Brigadier General Albert Pike tendered his resignation from the Confederate army. Pike was still feuding with General Hindman and denied that Hindman had any authority over Indian Territory or Pike's troops stationed there. Major General Theophilus C. Holmes of the Confederate high command took Hindman's side against Pike. Hindman immediately ordered Pike relieved of his command. The breakdown of the Confederate command in the Trans-Mississippi was painfully evident in its inaction in the Cherokee Nation in the face of the invasion by the Union Indian expedition.

After Chief John Ross ignored Colonel Weer's repeated attempts to meet with him, Captain Harris S. Greeno of the 6th Kansas Cavalry Regiment with one company of about sixty men from his regiment and fifty to a hundred Union Cherokees were sent with United States Indian Agents E. H. Carruth and H. W. Martin to contact Chief John Ross personally. Major William T. Campbell of the 6th Kansas Cavalry Regiment and a force of two hundred Union troops were also sent to capture Fort Gibson and to scout along the Arkansas River for Confederate troops. Campbell's force encountered no Confederate forces until it reached Fort Gibson, which Campbell captured on July 14, after skirmishing with the Confederate garrison of some forty to a hundred men. The Confederate force at Fort Gibson escaped across the Arkansas River to Cantonment Davis. Sources in Fort Gibson told Campbell that a force of six to seven thousand Rebels with two batteries of artillery under the command of General Albert Pike were gathered around Canton-

16. *OR*, XIII, 487–88.

ment Davis with plans to attack Colonel Weer's Union camps along the Grand River prairie. This, of course, was a gross exaggeration for Pike and his men were over one hundred miles to the south of Cantonment Davis. Major Campbell removed his forces to a pasture four miles north of Fort Gibson to graze his horses and rest his men because he could find no food or forage in the fort. Colonel Weer also had heard rumors of a possible Confederate attack on Campbell's force so he led an additional force of six hundred men to reinforce Campbell.[17]

On July 15 the combined force of Colonel Weer and Major Campbell reentered Fort Gibson unopposed. Campbell then led a scouting party three miles south of Fort Gibson to the bank of the Arkansas River across from Cantonment Davis. The Union party fired a few shots across the river, and the Confederate camp erupted in a hail of gunfire in the belief that Weer's Union expedition was attacking. The Union force had one man and one horse slightly injured in this gunfire before Major Campbell returned the troops to Fort Gibson and Weer withdrew his force by a "circuitous route" to his established camp on the Grand River.[18]

Captain Greeno's force occupied the Cherokee capital of Tahlequah on July 14 at about 5 P.M. after a twenty-two-mile ride. Captain Greeno, who before the war had been a physician, was an intelligent officer with good judgment and was an excellent choice to contact Chief Ross. Greeno's force surrounded Tahlequah and cautiously entered the Cherokee capital but found only four men. All the other male occupants had fled several days before amid rumors of an attack. Many of the women remaining in Tahlequah asked the Union soldiers to spare their men if they were captured. Greeno learned from a Negro that at Park Hill about two to three hundred Cherokees from Drew's regiment were still guarding Chief John Ross, his followers, and the village. Lieutenant Arch Scraper and a small force of men were also guarding the Cherokee officials, treasury, and government records. Chief Ross and his followers were living in fear of retaliation by Colonel Stand Watie's men for the recent mass defection by members of Drew's regiment and the Ross party to the Union camps. As best Captain Greeno could determine, the members of Drew's regiment at Park Hill were pro-Union and

17. *Ibid.*, 160–61.
18. *Ibid.*, 160.

also wished to join the Union invasion force, but they also wanted to protect Chief John Ross and his family. Greeno's force then rode two and one-half miles south of Tahlequah to Chapel Springs and camped for the night.[19]

On the morning of July 15, 1862, Captain Greeno sent Dr. Gilpatrick and three or four Union Indians to Park Hill to determine whether the members of Drew's regiment were really friendly to the Union side. Upon the receipt of positive information, Captain Greeno and his cavalry rode into Park Hill, where they were warmly greeted by the Ross party Cherokees gathered there. At Chief Ross's home Lieutenant Colonel William P. Ross, Major Thomas Pegg, Lieutenant Anderson Benge, Lieutenant Joseph Chover, Lieutenant Lacy Hawkins, Lieutenant Archibald Scraper, Lieutenant Walter Chuster, Lieutenant George W. Ross (one of Chief Ross's sons), Lieutenant Allen Ross (another son of Chief Ross, who was a sergeant when mustered in), Lieutenant Joseph Cornsilk, Lieutenant John Shell, and various enlisted men of Drew's regiment greeted them.[20]

The men of Drew's regiment at Park Hill had received orders just a few hours earlier from Colonel Douglas H. Cooper to report to his headquarters at Cantonment Davis. Chief John Ross had likewise received orders from Cooper, who in the name of Confederate President Jefferson Davis issued a proclamation calling for all Cherokee males between the ages of eighteen and thirty-five to take up arms to repel the Union invasion of their homeland. General Pike also sent a letter to Chief Ross asking to borrow $50,000 in gold from the Cherokee treasury to add to another $50,000 from the Confederate government to pay those Cherokees still "true to the alliance of the Cherokee government and true to the alliance of the Cherokee people with the Confederate States."[21]

Lieutenant Colonel Ross hesitated to make a decision concerning his command so Captain Greeno placed him and his officers under arrest as prisoners of war, much to the relief of the remaining Cherokees in Drew's regiment. Chief John Ross was also placed under arrest. Thus the old chief was relieved of ordering his people to arms to fight the Federals because under the Cherokee treaty with the

19. *Ibid.*, 161–62; Commissioner of Indian Affairs, *Report of the Commissioner of Indian Affairs for the Year 1862* (Washington, D.C., 1863), 158.
20. *OR*, XIII, 162.
21. Pike to Drew, July 14, 1862, in Foreman Papers, Gilcrease Institute.

Confederate States of America he was obliged to furnish men when called to do so by the Confederate government. Chief Ross was immediately paroled by the Union force.

Chief Ross and his followers, however, were badly frightened, fearing that Colonel Watie and his men would pounce on them for being so willingly captured by the Union forces and so quickly paroled. Captain Greeno spoke to the two hundred Cherokee soldiers from Drew's regiment at Park Hill about joining the Union army. He told the assembled Cherokees that the Union Indian expedition had more than two thousand men and many cannon ready to fight the Confederates. He said the Federal government had not deserted its Indian friends, but it had taken a long time to organize its forces so it could chase away the Confederates who occupied the Cherokee Nation. Captain Greeno spoke about how Major General Ulysses S. Grant's army had driven the Confederates out of Kentucky and defeated them at Fort Henry, Fort Donelson, and more recently at Shiloh. He also explained that the Confederate forts had fallen at Island No. 10 on the upper Mississippi River with the Union capturing three Confederate generals, five thousand soldiers, and more than a hundred cannon, and that the mighty Union navy had destroyed the Confederate ram flotilla at Memphis, Tennessee. Greeno reminded the Cherokees of their recent defeat at Pea Ridge and told them the Union had captured New Orleans, cutting the Confederacy in half except for a small stretch of the Mississippi River still held by the Confederates between Vicksburg and Port Hudson. It would be only a matter of time, Greeno said, before additional Union victories would result in conquering the entire Confederacy.[22]

In ending his speech, Greeno said the Union was firm but conciliatory and did not want to take revenge on the Cherokees for their past deeds. Those Cherokees who had gone over to the Confederate side in response to threats and promises of the Confederate government and had fought against the Union would be forgiven if, convinced of their previous error, they now joined with the Union. The Union would restore all loyal Indians to their homes and do all in its power to protect them.[23]

The Ross party Cherokees were strongly moved by Captain

22. Britton, *Union Indian Brigade*, 69–72.
23. *Ibid.*

Greeno's speech, and many men in Drew's regiment expressed a desire to go with the Union troops and enter their army. Chief Ross also aided the Union force as much as possible, even revealing the location of Confederate stores and ammunition buried nearby. Undoubtedly a number of Union Cherokees joined Greeno in trying to convince the rest of the Ross party Cherokees to join the Union.[24]

Greeno's force camped at Park Hill that night and left for its base camp on July 16, 1862. When Greeno's soldiers left Park Hill, they were accompanied by Chief Ross, his family, and two hundred recruits for the newly formed 3d Kansas Indian Home Guard Regiment, for which the Reverend John Buttrick Jones now served as chaplain. The Pins raided the farms of the Southern sympathizers in the area, freeing slaves and taking livestock and supplies. Greeno's force arrived at camp at four o'clock that afternoon.[25]

Hearing rumors of mass desertions to the Union invaders by members of the Ross party, Colonel Douglas H. Cooper ordered all of Drew's men true to the South to join Colonel Drew at his headquarters "immediately—Our friends must separate themselves & come out from the enemy." Cooper stated that those Cherokees who failed to show up would be treated as deserters. In a letter to Drew, Cooper said, "I think your Regt ought to rally & show to the world that they are not on the side of the north." Colonel Cooper also wanted Lieutenant Colonel Ross and his uncle, Chief John Ross, to withdraw from Park Hill to a place of safety. Once again, however, the Confederate high command acted too late.[26]

General Albert Pike later wrote that Chief Ross "considered his life in danger from his own people, in consequence of their ancient feud, he allowed himself to be taken prisoner by the Federal troops. At the time, I believed that if white troops had been sent to Park Hill, who would have protected him against Watie's men, he would have remained at home and adhered to the Confederate States, voluntarily entered into,—true at heart and in his inmost soul,—or else he is falser and more treacherous than I can believe him to be."[27]

Chief John Ross and his followers were now firmly in the Union camp. Drew's regiment, except for a small body of men led by Cap-

24. *OR*, XIII, 162.

25. Linda Finley, "Notes from the Diary of Susan E. Foreman," *Chronicles of Oklahoma*, XLVII (Winter, 1969–70), 397.

26. Cooper to Drew, July 18, 1862, in Foreman Papers, Gilcrease Institute.

27. Abel, *American Indian as Participant*, 139.

tain Pickens M. Benge and a few other officers, including Colonel
John Drew, became the nucleus of the 3d Kansas Indian Home
Guard Regiment.[28] Colonel John Drew wrote Colonel Cooper that
he was unable to leave his home at Webbers Falls because there were
fifteen cases of measles in his family and he himself felt ill. Drew had
no communication with Chief Ross and the portions of his regiment
at Tahlequah and Park Hill. Drew had not been in the northern area
of the Cherokee Nation to unite his regiment against the Union
invasion. Further to crush Cooper's optimism, Drew stated that he
had heard that a pro-Union company of Cherokees was being organized on the Canadian River in the southwest corner of the Cherokee Nation and they intended to go north to join the Union invasion force. Colonel Drew sent Captain Porum Davis to check out the
rumor.[29]

Those Cherokees remaining in the Cherokee Nation had to do
some serious soul-searching to decide on which side their allegiance
should lie. The presence of both armies in the Cherokee Nation
reinforced the fact that they faced a life-or-death situation. Some
Cherokees, however, still hoped to remain neutral. George M. Murrell wrote on July 23, 1862, while in exile at Van Buren, Arkansas, "It
is a miserable way of living and I am tired of it but do not feel
inclined to return without I go with an army." There were to be no
neutrals among the Cherokees.[30]

Meanwhile, the white Northern troops began to fear that a Confederate raid might capture their badly needed supply trains and cut
them off from Union posts in Kansas. No rain had fallen since the
Union Indian expedition's entrance into the Cherokee Nation, and
the troops were sweltering in the heat. Supplies were running low,
and many of the new white soldiers were on the verge of mutiny in
their desire to return to civilized Kansas.

The Union expedition was down to only three days of rations and
had had no communication with the Union forces in Kansas for
twelve days. Weer sent three different sets of couriers to Kansas, but
all failed to report back to him. A wagon train from Kansas was
expected for three days but had not appeared. It seems that at first
Colonel Weer decided to follow the advice of his officers' council and
withdraw to a point closer to Kansas. He then changed his mind,

28. *OR*, XIII, 40.
29. Cooper to Drew, July 20, 1862, in Foreman Papers, Gilcrease Institute.
30. George Murrell to Tim, July 23, 1862, *ibid.*

ordered his troops put on half rations, and told them to stay put. Reports of Confederate forces marching up the Verdigris River to cut off the Union force from Kansas (reports greatly exaggerated) frightened Colonel Frederick Salomon into taking an action that would lose much of what Colonel Weer and the Union force had so boldly gained. On July 18, 1862, just when the entire Cherokee Nation was about to fall to the Federal invasion force without another shot being fired, Salomon arrested Colonel William Weer. Salomon alleged that Weer had led his Union invasion force so deep into enemy territory that they were now in danger of being cut off and destroyed by the Confederates. Salomon also charged Weer with refusing the advice of his military council and leading the expedition 160 miles from its main base of operations in Kansas and with being abusive to fellow officers and drinking while on duty. Salomon later wrote, "I could but conclude that the man was either insane, premeditated treachery to his troops or perhaps that his grossly intemperate habits long continued had produced idiocy or monomania."[31]

Colonel Salomon took over command of the invasion force as next in command and quickly ordered all of the white units to withdraw to Union bases in Kansas except for a section of Captain Allen's 1st Kansas Battery. The evening of July 18, 1862, a courier reached Salomon with the news that the long-awaited Union supply train was at Hudson's Crossing some seventy-five miles to the north awaiting an escort. The Union force began its retrograde march to Kansas on July 19, the day after Colonel Weer's arrest. Colonel Salomon heard additional rumors that Watie and twelve hundred Confederates were marching up the east side of the Grand River to attack the Union wagon train so Salomon marched back up the Fort Scott–Fort Gibson Military Road toward Fort Scott to ensure the safety of his long-awaited supply train. The three regiments of Kansas Indian Home Guard in Colonel Robert W. Furnas' Union Indian Brigade were left to hold what territory they could in the Cherokee Nation. An advance detachment of two hundred men of the 1st Kansas Indian Home Guard was stationed at Vann's Ford on the Verdigris River to guard it from Confederate forces, and two hundred men of the 3d Kansas Indian Home Guard were at Fort Gibson under Major John A. Foreman guarding crossings on the Arkansas and Grand rivers. Colonel Furnas ordered the Indian regiments to

31. *OR*, XIII, 475–77, 484–85.

encamp on the Verdigris River at Camp Corwin to consolidate them into a united force.[32]

The Union force had been in the Cherokee Nation about a month, and hundreds of refugee Indians had returned to their farms, believing that they would be protected by the Union forces under Colonel Weer. With the bulk of the white troops now encamped in Kansas or on their way there under Colonel Salomon, the recently returned loyal Indians were now vulnerable to Confederate raids. The Union Indians were again on the defensive and were afraid Colonel Douglas H. Cooper and his army of Texans, Cherokees, Creeks, Seminoles, Choctaws, and Chickasaws would sweep down on the outnumbered Union Indian regiments and drive them from the Cherokee Nation. Such action would leave the loyal Indian families to be dealt with by the Confederates as they pleased.[33]

The Union officers of the Indian regiments met at 8 P.M. on July 19, 1862, to plan what steps were necessary to hold the Cherokee Nation. Part of the 1st and 2d Indian Home Guard regiments contained soldiers who lived in the area of the Verdigris River near where the bulk of the Indian regiments were camped. Lacking the support of the white regiments and feeling abandoned by the Union, some of these Union Indians deserted from their regiments and went home. Colonel Furnas, commander of the Union Indian Brigade, finally ordered the 3d Kansas Indian Home Guard Regiment, led by Major William A. Phillips, to camp on Pryor Creek to avoid the demoralization suffered by the other two regiments and also to obtain good water and forage.

Some 180 Osages in a company of the 2d Kansas Indian Home Guard Regiment deserted their unit to go buffalo hunting. On July 23, 1862, the Union Indian Brigade was ordered to move northward and camp near Horse Creek, twenty miles below Hudson's Ferry at Camp Wattles on the Fort Scott–Fort Gibson Military Road to hold what territory they could in the Cherokee Nation. Meager verbal and indefinite written orders were given to the Union Indian regiments by Colonel Salomon before he quickly departed from the Indian nations, and thus Colonel Furnas and his officers were at a loss as to what to do.[34]

The sudden retreat of the bulk of the Federal forces took everyone

32. *Ibid.*, 481, 485.
33. Britton, *Union Indian Brigade*, 73–74.
34. *OR*, XIII, 511–12; Britton, *Civil War on the Border*, 310.

by surprise, especially the Ross party Cherokees. The new Union recruits from John Drew's regiment were now left to fend for themselves along with the other Union Indians. The bulk of the white forces that fled north were soon followed by Indian refugees who had earlier fled with Opothleyahola and the new refugees who had earlier followed the South. Both the Confederate and Union troops ravaged much of the countryside, sacking homes of Indians on both sides and laying waste to farms and ranches. Many former slaves were also scouring the countryside securing food and shelter wherever they could. Anarchy existed in the Cherokee Nation, where the rule of law was now replaced by the rule of the rifle and tomahawk.[35]

On July 30, 1862, Major General Thomas C. Hindman took control of the Trans-Mississippi District. Major General Holmes, who was a friend of General Hindman, continued quarreling with Brigadier General Albert Pike and transferred all of Pike's white forces out of Fort McCulloch and refused to send Pike any more supplies.

On August 3, 1862, part of Colonel William F. Cloud's 6th Kansas Cavalry Regiment escorted about a dozen carriages carrying Chief John Ross, his family, $70,000 to $90,000 in the Cherokee treasury, and the Cherokee archives from Park Hill to Baxter Springs, Kansas, where Chief Ross made a short speech to some Cherokee refugees and soldiers promising to defend their rights and to preserve the Cherokee Nation. Chief Ross and his party proceeded to Fort Scott, where he was greeted by General James G. Blunt. About thirty-seven Cherokees traveled with Chief Ross, and Company F of the 3d Kansas Indian Home Guard Regiment served as his bodyguard.[36]

Chief Ross then made arrangements for exile among his wife's relatives in Philadelphia. A number of Cherokees, however, remained in the Park Hill area, where Chief Ross's brother Lewis Ross tried to keep them supplied with food. The pro-Union Cherokees remaining in the Cherokee Nation feared that Watie's raiders would reap retribution on them, and soon their worst fears were realized.[37]

Part of the 1st Kansas Indian Home Guard Regiment was sent after the group of Osage deserters from the Union regiments, and that Union force ran into a group of 125 Confederates on the Ver-

35. Bahos, "John Ross," 124, 125.
36. Commissioner of Indian Affairs, *Report, 1862*, 160–62.
37. *OR*, XIII, 512.

digris River. The Confederate force captured 14 Union soldiers and 1 Osage deserter in the encounter. The Union prisoners were sent to Cantonment Davis. In disgust over the way the white Union troops had fled from the Cherokee Nation, more of the Indian regiments went home without leave, but these soldiers later returned to their units when sent for by their officers.[38]

Major William A. Phillips, commander of the 1st Kansas Indian Home Guard Regiment, marched his command to Tahlequah and Park Hill to try to protect the remaining Loyal Cherokees from Colonel Stand Watie's nearby forces. William Phillips was born in Scotland and arrived in the United States in 1839. He lived in Illinois, became a newspaperman, and moved to Kansas in 1855 as a correspondent of the New York *Tribune*. There he became involved in abolitionist activities. On March 29, 1862, Phillips became a major in the 1st Kansas Indian Home Guard Regiment.[39]

Major Phillips sent his command out from Park Hill after hearing of the Confederate raiders' intentions. His regiment of Union Cherokees advanced down the three different roads that converged at Bayou Menard (also called Bayou Bernard) about seven miles northeast of Fort Gibson in search of the Confederate force reported to be in the area. Colonel Watie's regiment and parts of several other Confederate units had crossed the Arkansas River near Cantonment Davis to take revenge on the Cherokee traitors who had switched their allegiance to the United States. On July 27, 1862, the 3d Kansas Indian Home Guard Regiment ran into Lieutenant Colonel Thomas Fox Taylor and four hundred Confederate Cherokees of Watie's regiment marching from Fort Gibson to Park Hill on the Park Hill Fork. Lieutenant John S. Haneway, in charge of the right wing of Phillips' force, fought a delaying action while retreating toward Park Hill as the other two Union parties advanced on Taylor's force down the other roads. Phillips' Union force converged along the three different roads that ultimately joined into a fork, but the Confederates thought the Union force was coming down only one road so they concentrated all their men there and were drawn down it without posting any rear guard. Major Phillips' other troops stormed

38. Muster Roll, Co. C, 2d Kansas Indian Home Guard Regiment, July–August, 1862, Compiled Records Showing Service of Military Units in Volunteer Union Organizations, Microcopy 594, roll 225, National Archives Microfilm Publications, Washington, D.C.

39. Britton, *Union Indian Brigade*, 74.

down the other two roads upon hearing the sounds of battle from Lieutenant Haneway's force and turned the unprotected Confederate flanks. The Confederates, taken by surprise, were surrounded by the three detachments of Union Cherokees and routed in what was known as the Battle of Bayou Menard. Twenty-five Confederates were captured and 32 bodies were found in the fields after the battle. Total Confederate losses were reported to be 125. Among the dead were Lieutenant Colonel Thomas Fox Taylor and Captain Hicks of Watie's regiment, as well as two Choctaw captains. Major Phillips' regiment had but one casualty, a severely wounded private. Phillips then marched his command back to the Union camp at Flat Rock Creek near the Grand River.[40]

During the Battle of Bayou Menard, another part of Colonel Watie's regiment was twenty miles away encircling Union Major Foreman's camp on the Grand River. Foreman's Union Creeks refused to fight so Foreman was forced to retreat with his artillery without putting up much of a fight.[41]

Colonel Salomon was promoted to brigadier general shortly after assuming command of the Indian expedition and deposing Colonel William Weer. General Blunt, as department commander, sent Weer orders to hold the Cherokee Nation from a point a few miles above Fort Gibson on the west side of the Grand River. Salomon, however, felt that such an order was not reasonable because Weer's command would be 180 miles from its supply base at Fort Scott, Kansas, so he chose to ignore it. If his lines of communication were cut by the Confederates, he believed the Union expedition would be trapped without food or ammunition. No major roads led to Union territory except the Texas Road or the Fort Scott–Fort Gibson Military Road along the Grand River. Food was very scarce in the Indian nations because of the strife and previous foraging by both sides. There was not enough to feed both the Union troops and the refugee Indians in many portions of the occupied Cherokee Nation unless supply trains from the North could reach the area. For these reasons Salomon decided to save the white Union troops and to let the Union Indians fend for themselves. Obviously Salomon had little interest in the fate of the Union Indians.

Salomon finally retreated to Camp Quapaw in the Quapaw Na-

40. Britton, *Civil War on the Border*, 310–11; *OR*, XIII, 181–84.
41. *OR*, XIII, 183–84.

tion just south of the Kansas line with the bulk of the Union expedition. Colonel Furnas' Union Indian Brigade was now headquartered at Wolf Creek about forty-five miles south of Camp Quapaw with three separate detachments scattered along the Fort Scott–Fort Gibson Military Road at key crossings. The Indian regiments were also continually scouting the Cherokee Nation for Confederate raiders.[42]

The Union Indian regiments had suffered large losses from the recent desertions, and they retreated without provisions up the Fort Scott–Fort Gibson Road toward Fort Scott. Their camps during the retreat were at Chouteau's, Alberty's, Wolf Creek, Sulphur Springs, Horse Creek, Hudson's Crossing, Spring River, and finally Camp Corwin on the Spring River. Only some twelve hundred Indians in the three regiments were available for duty when they finally reached the Kansas border.[43]

There were few Union troops in southwestern Missouri at this time and Confederate forces periodically rode through that area to threaten Kansas and the Union posts to the north along the Missouri River. General Samuel R. Curtis' army, which had been in northwestern Arkansas, was in eastern Arkansas at Helena on the Mississippi River and was of no aid in the Union defense of Kansas or western Missouri. On August 11, 1862, Confederate Colonel John T. Hughes led a raiding party of some eight hundred Confederates to occupy the Union-held town of Independence, Missouri. He defeated more than three hundred Union soldiers there after a sharp fight and forced them to surrender the town. This Confederate victory in the heart of Union territory caused turmoil in Kansas and Missouri. Independence was only a few miles east of strategic Kansas City on the road to St. Louis and Jefferson City.[44]

Not only were Union lines of communication from Kansas to the East threatened, but those between Fort Leavenworth and Fort Scott were exposed to the Confederate raiders. General Blunt quickly decided that the Indian expedition had more pressing matters to attend to in Kansas and Missouri than in the Cherokee Nation and rushed from Fort Leavenworth to Fort Scott, where Brigadier General Frederick Salomon's force had just arrived after a forced march

42. *Ibid.*, 521.
43. Muster Roll, Co. A, 2d Kansas Indian Home Guard Regiment, July–August, 1862, Microcopy 594, roll 225, National Archives Microfilm Publications.
44. *OR*, XIII, 225–32.

from Baxter Springs. General Blunt took command of all available Union forces at Fort Scott and made a forced march through southwestern Missouri to Lone Jack, Missouri, where he confronted four thousand Confederates who had just beaten a force of about six hundred Union Missouri militia at Lone Jack on August 16, 1862.[45]

The Confederate raiders escaped Blunt's exhausted force in a blinding rainstorm, but Blunt's men chased the Confederates into northwestern Arkansas without much contact and with very few losses. This campaign of forced marches totally exhausted the Union troops of the former Indian expedition. Most of the horses of the Union cavalry were unserviceable and unfit for future action. The three Kansas Indian Home Guard regiments and some white troops and artillery were left in camp on the west side of the Grand River only a few miles south of Baxter Springs. The Confederate raid on Independence, Missouri, appears to have kept Brigadier General Salomon from a possible court-martial because his troops arrived at Fort Scott just when General Blunt needed them. Nor were charges ever brought against Colonel William Weer on Salomon's accusations against him. The Union army apparently chose to ignore the retreat of the Union white troops from the Cherokee Nation.[46]

Thus ended the first Union invasion of the Indian nations. The rift between the Ross party and Ridge party Cherokees was now as wide as the Grand Canyon. Drew's regiment was dissolved with most of its members in Union Indian regiments and a few still fighting on the side of the Confederacy. Guerrilla warfare raged throughout the Cherokee Nation as it became a hotbed of outlaws, renegades, and vigilantes from both sides.

45. *Ibid.*, 235–39.
46. Britton, *Union Indian Brigade*, 75–79.

Epilogue

A second Union invasion of the Cherokee Nation began in late 1862, and the decisive Union victory at the Battle of Honey Springs on July 17, 1863, sealed the fate of the Confederate forces in the Indian nations. The Cherokees in the 2d and 3d Kansas Indian Home Guard regiments played important roles in most battles in the Indian nations as well as in a few battles in Missouri and Arkansas. The deserters from Drew's regiment received very little sympathy from Watie's Cherokees, and many were killed when captured. Civil war continued to rage through the Cherokee Nation and the other Indian nations until Brigadier General Stand Watie became the last Confederate general to surrender to Federal authorities on June 23, 1865.

After Drew's regiment broke up in July, 1862, Colonel John Drew continued his service in the Confederate army as an officer at the post of Cantonment Davis.[1] Colonel Drew and a company of men were at Chief John Ross's home in late 1862, at Park Hill near where Union troops had destroyed the home of Lewis Ross, Chief Ross's brother.[2] Drew continued to make salt for the Confederacy from his salt works until they, too, were confiscated by the Confederacy as a vital resource in the war effort. It was reported that Drew did not consider the payments of $400 per month from the Confederate government for the manufacture of salt sufficient compensation.[3]

As the Confederacy's fortunes waned in the Indian nations, Colonel John Drew became a soldier without a command, not trusted by either side. When the second Federal invasion force entered the Cherokee Nation and occupied most of the Cherokee lands, Colonel Drew sent "overtures of peace" to Colonel William A. Phillips, now commander of the Union Indian Brigade of Kansas Indian Home Guard Regiments, which still included many former members of

---

1. J. W. Wells to Drew, July 29, 1862, in Drew Papers, 62-58.
2. Alice Robertson Collection, 1862-122, University of Tulsa, Tulsa, Oklahoma.
3. Affidavit of Thomas Lunigan, October 16, 1862, in Drew Papers, 62-60.

Drew's regiment. On August 25, 1865, Colonel John Drew died a very poor and a very sad man in a land ravaged by war.[4]

After his arrest by the Union troops under Captain Greeno, Lieutenant Colonel William P. Ross went north under parole with his uncle, Chief John Ross, and other members of the Ross party and family. In 1863 William P. Ross returned to Fort Gibson to run a sutler's store for the 3d Kansas Indian Home Guard Regiment. He helped prevent many of the pro-Union Cherokee refugees in the Fort Gibson area from starving to death by bringing them food and supplies on his own account. One night in the summer of 1863 his sutler's store was burned to the ground, and he and his firm lost $30,000 worth of goods. In late 1863 William P. Ross was captured by Colonel Stand Watie, but Watie did not kill him because he had promised his wife, Sarah Watie, to preserve Ross's life for the sake of Ross's mother.[5]

Unlike most members of Drew's regiment, William P. Ross did not take up arms against the Confederacy, and he did his best to stay neutral. Ross was chosen by the Cherokee National Council to become principal chief of the Cherokee Nation in November, 1866, to replace his uncle, Chief John Ross, upon the elder Ross's death. Unlike most military officers, William Ross did not keep his title of lieutenant colonel after the war. The Ross party later split, with some members supporting William P. Ross and others supporting the Reverend Lewis Downing. After Chief Lewis Downing's death in 1873, William P. Ross again became principal chief of the Cherokee Nation. Ross died on July 28, 1891, at the age of seventy-one.[6]

Major Thomas Pegg also fled north with the pro-Union Indians and Ross party Cherokees. After his departure from Drew's regiment, Pegg enlisted as an officer in the 2d Kansas Indian Home Guard Regiment and became the captain of Company A. In February, 1863, at Camp John Ross on Cowskin Prairie in the Cherokee Nation Major Pegg was elected president of the pro-Union Cherokee Council. This council declared the August 21, 1861, treaty between the Confederate States of America and the Cherokee Nation void because it was "entered into under duress" and had "no

4. Daniel Ross to Charlotte Drew, August 27, 1862, *ibid.*, 65-75.
5. Dale and Litton (eds.), *Cherokee Cavaliers*, 129, 144.
6. John Bartlett Meserve, "Chief William Potter Ross," *Chronicles of Oklahoma*, XV (March, 1938), 24.

binding effect, either in law or morals." Pegg was elected assistant principal chief of the pro-Union Cherokees and acted as chief while Chief John Ross lived in exile in Washington, D.C., and Philadelphia during the remainder of the Civil War. Colonel Stand Watie, meanwhile, was elected principal chief of the Cherokees by the pro-Confederate faction of Cherokees and later became a Confederate brigadier general.[7]

The chaplain of Drew's regiment, the Reverend Lewis Downing, became the lieutenant colonel of the Union 3d Kansas Indian Home Guard Regiment, and he presided over the Union Cherokee Council held at Camp John Ross in February, 1863, at Cowskin Prairie. This was the council that elected Thomas Pegg as principal chief in Chief John Ross's absence. The council under Downing pledged its loyalty to the government of the United States of America, freed all Cherokee slaves, and ordered the removal from office of all Cherokee officials not loyal to the United States government.[8]

Lieutenant Colonel Lewis Downing went to Washington, D.C., in 1863 to plead for assistance for the Cherokees from the United States government. He later represented the Cherokees at Fort Smith, Arkansas, in 1865 and at another conference with United States peace commissioners and other negotiators in 1866 on the new Cherokee treaty. After Chief John Ross's death, the Reverend Lewis Downing, assistant principal chief, became the acting principal chief of the Cherokee Nation until William P. Ross was chosen to fill the unexpired term of his uncle on October 19, 1866. Downing supported equal rights for all Cherokees and set up a party known as the Downing party, which included both Ross party and Ridge party supporters and represented the political reality among the Cherokees. Some members of the Ross party, as well as William P. Ross, supported the exclusion of all Confederate Cherokees from tribal office. Lewis Downing was later elected principal chief of the Cherokee Nation and served in that capacity until his death on November 9, 1872. He was instrumental in bringing together the Ross and Ridge factions.[9]

Israel G. Vore, the quartermaster of Drew's regiment, stayed in the Confederate army and became a major in the Confederate quar-

7. Delegates of the Cherokee Nation, *Memorial to the President*.
8. Grant Foreman, *A History of Oklahoma* (Norman, 1945), 115.
9. John Bartlett Meserve, "Chief Lewis Downing and Chief Charles Thompson (Oochalata)," *Chronicles of Oklahoma*, XVI (September, 1938), 319–20.

termaster corps. In May, 1863, Vore was appointed the Confederate Creek agent. After the Civil War Vore engaged in many matters for the Creek Nation and continued to raise cattle and to preach.[10]

Other officers in Drew's regiment suffered various fates. Captain George Scraper, who deserted to Opothleyahola's forces before the Battle of Caving Banks, joined the 2d Kansas Indian Home Guard Regiment before the invasion of the Cherokee Nation by the Indian expedition. Captain Scraper was killed in action on September 20, 1862, while leading his Company H in a fight at Shirley's Ford on the Spring River in Missouri.[11]

Another deserter at Caving Banks, Captain James McDaniel, was the company commander of Company A of the 2d Kansas Indian Home Guard Regiment and served through the war. In 1866 James McDaniel served as a Cherokee delegate on a Federal commission to Washington, D.C. He died in 1867 in Washington and was reportedly buried in Arlington National Cemetery.[12]

James S. Vann, the former adjutant of Drew's regiment, became commander of Company A of the 3d Kansas Indian Home Guard Regiment. Vann is also reported to be buried in Arlington National Cemetery. Captain Richard Fields, who was captured by the Union at Pea Ridge, imprisoned, and later paroled, returned home to a divided Cherokee Nation. Captain Fields continued to serve the Confederate army as an officer in Colonel Stand Watie's command. Fields visited Richmond, Virginia, in 1864, bringing letters from various Indian leaders in an effort to get more help from the Confederate government. He proposed to raise a battalion of partisan rangers in February, 1864, to fight the Union but does not appear to have done so. After the war Richard Fields was active in representing the Confederate Cherokees during peace treaty negotiations with the United States.[13] The brave Captain Pickens Benge, who kept some of his men from deserting at Caving Banks, continued his service in the Confederate forces after the breakup of Drew's regiment. Captain Benge was wounded on August 24, 1862, and died during the winter of 1863.[14]

10. Foreman, "Israel G. Vore," 201, 203.
11. *OR,* XIII, 278.
12. Muriel H. Wright, "Colonel Cooper's Civil War Report on the Battle of Round Mountain," *Chronicles of Oklahoma,* XXXIX (Winter, 1961–62), 366.
13. Dale and Litton (eds.), *Cherokee Cavaliers,* 226–27; Wardell, *Political History,* 208–209, 211.
14. Hicks, "Diary," 8.

Two of Chief John Ross's sons who served in Drew's regiment, Allen Ross and George W. Ross, were joined by others of Chief Ross's sons, James and Silas, as members of the 3d Indian Home Guard Regiment. James Ross was captured by Confederates while bringing supplies to his family at Park Hill in 1862 and died in a Confederate prison in 1864. Chief Ross's other sons survived the war.[15]

Among the pallbearers at Chief John Ross's funeral were Colonel William A. Phillips, Captain White Catcher, Captain James Mc-Daniel, Captain Smith Christie, Lieutenant Samuel Houston Benge, Daniel H. Ross, and the Reverend John B. Jones. Captain White Catcher was commander of Company I, Captain Smith Christie was commander of Company A, and Lieutenant Samuel Houston Benge was also in Company A of the 3d Kansas Indian Home Guard Regiment.[16]

Some 2,200 Cherokees fought on the Union side during the Civil War. A total of 3,530 men from the Indian nations served in the Union army, and 1,018 of that number died during their enlistment. Thus 28.8 percent or more than one-fourth of all Indians in the Union army died of disease, were killed in battle, or died of wounds. No state had a higher percentage of losses than the Indian nations.[17]

A census of the Union Cherokees in 1863 showed that one-third of the adult women were widows and one-fourth of the children were orphans. The situation was similar for the Confederate Cherokees, who also suffered heavily during the conflict. By the war's end the Cherokees were almost destitute. Guerrilla war, outlaws, and prof-iteering by members of both sides left little of value to the Cherokees.[18]

A census of the Cherokee Nation in 1867 showed only a popula-tion of 13,566 as compared to 21,000 in 1860. This loss of about 7,000 or about one-third of the Cherokee people is an indication of the death, destruction, and consequent alienation that the Civil War brought the Cherokee Nation.[19]

In 1868 and 1869, the Confederate Cherokees returned to the

15. Moulton, *John Ross*, 177.
16. Foreman Papers, Box 37, Gilcrease Institute.
17. Francis Trevelyan Miller (ed.), *The Photographic History of the Civil War* (10 vols.; New York, 1957), X, 146.
18. Wardell, *Political History*, 175.
19. Mooney, "Myths of the Cherokee," 149.

Cherokee Nation after having lived in exile in the Choctaw Nation, Chickasaw Nation, and Texas. Some loyal Indians, especially Creeks, remained in the Cherokee Nation after the Civil War out of fear of reprisals by their Confederate tribesmen for their actions during the war. As late as 1869 a number of Creeks were moved back to the Creek Nation from the Cherokee Nation.[20]

Although Drew's regiment did not survive its scheduled year of Confederate service, it left an enduring mark in the history of the American Civil War as the only Confederate regiment to have almost its entire membership desert into Union service. Those Cherokees who survived the war were faced with the reconstruction of a ravaged homeland and the healing of many wounds left by the war. The officers of Drew's regiment played a key role in mending a torn Cherokee Nation and dealing with the white infringements upon their lands in the years after the Civil War before the final opening of Indian lands to white settlement and the formation of the state of Oklahoma.

20. Bailey, *Reconstruction in Indian Territory,* 35.

Appendix I
Muster Roll of Officers of Drew's Regiment on November 5, 1861

FIELD AND STAFF

Colonel John Drew
Lieutenant Colonel William Potter Ross
Major Thomas Pegg
Adjutant James S. Vann
A. Quartermaster Israel G. Vore
A. C. S. Frederick Augustus Kerr
Surgeon James P. Evans
Chaplain Reverend Lewis Downing
Assistant Surgeon Joseph W. Carden

OFFICERS

Company A

Captain Jefferson D. Hicks
First Lieutenant Anderson Benge
Second Lieutenant Ah mer cher ner
Second Lieutenant Lacy Hawkins

Company B

Captain Nicholas B. Sanders
First Lieutenant White Catcher
Second Lieutenant George O. Sanders
Second Lieutenant Josiah Deer in the Water

Company C

Captain John Porum Davis
First Lieutenant Samuel H. Smith
Second Lieutenant Deer in the Water Star
Second Lieutenant Charles Drew

Company D

Captain Isaac N. Hildebrand
First Lieutenant George Springston
Second Lieutenant Samuel Runaway
Second Lieutenant Ezekiel Russell

Company E

Captain James Vann
First Lieutenant Eli Smith
Second Lieutenant Christy Chicken toater
Second Lieutenant Fogg

Company F

Captain Richard Fields
First Lieutenant John Young
Second Lieutenant Broom Baldridge
Second Lieutenant William Webber

Company G

Captain George W. Scraper
First Lieutenant Jesse Henry
Second Lieutenant Arch Scraper
Second Lieutenant Joseph Chu wee

Company H

Captain Edward R. Hicks
First Lieutenant Nathaniel Fish
Second Lieutenant George W. Ross
Second Lieutenant Samuel Downing

Company I

Captain Albert Pike
First Lieutenant Samuel Foster
Second Lieutenant Red Little / Redbird / Little Bird
Second Lieutenant John Bear Meat

Company K

Captain Pickens M. Benge
First Lieutenant George Benge
Second Lieutenant Trotting Wolf
Second Lieutenant Crab Grass Smith

McDaniel's or 1st Reserve Company

Captain James McDaniel
First Lieutenant Watt Stop
Second Lieutenant Big Sky yah too kah / Skieyaltooka
Second Lieutenant Noah Drowning Bear

Source: Compiled Service Records of Confederate Soldiers Who Served in Organizations Raised Directly by the Confederate Government, Microcopy 258, Rolls 77 and
78, National Archives Microfilm Publications, Washington, D.C.

Appendix II
Muster Roll of Drew's Regiment on November 5, 1861

Name	Age	Company
Pvt. Adam (a Creek)	30	K
Pvt. Adam	19	McD
Sgt. George Adams	35	B
Pvt. Ae tor he	48	H
Pvt. Ah gah yah skie	25	F
Pvt. Ah hool ota ke Pouch	22	I
Pvt. Ah hur too kat	37	I
Pvt. Ah ker loo ker	30	A
Pvt. Ah kil lu ne gah	46	E
Pvt. Ah lay oh ie	35	F
Cpl. Ah le cher	26	A
Cpl. Ah le cher	25	E
Pvt. Ah le kee w nah soo zee	19	G
Pvt. Ah le whe ter	21	A
Pvt. Ah mah soo yah Tee cah cah husky	32	I
Lt. Ah mer Cher ner	30	A
Pvt. Ah mi ye har	23	H
Pvt. Ah na ne yeh skie	21	G
Pvt. Ah nee chee	27	E
Pvt. Ahquahta Kie	60	D
Pvt. Charles Ah que che	29	G
Pvt. Ah Sah lah tee skie	33	G
Pvt. John Ah sto le te	22	A
Pvt. Ah Coo wah Ah taw hee	27	D
Pvt. Ah tawhee Ah Coowah	27	D
Pvt. Ah tsa de hie	36	F
Pvt. Ah yun too kah	18	McD
Pvt. Aleck	20	F
Pvt. Watt Allbones	30	A

Name	Age	Company
Pvt. Ar chil lar	30	F
Pvt. Ar chiller Peach Eater	18	K
Pvt. Archy / Archie	20	A
Pvt. Ark tae hae skie	30	H
Pvt. Ar le cha	32	H
Pvt. Art lan se ne	20	H
Pvt. Joseph Ashes	23	C
Pvt. Joseph Ash hopper	21	E
Pvt. William Ash hopper	34	E
Pvt. A-to-la he	30	B
Pvt. A tun hee	31	C
Pvt. Avc Tah le yas Kie	27	K
Pvt. A wie	21	E
Pvt. James Bagg	—	C
Pvt. Ave Baldridge	42	A
Lt. Broom Baldridge	60	F
Killed at Caving Banks		
Pvt. Columbus Baldridge	37	B
Pvt. Dick Baldridge	56	C
Sgt. James Baldridge	47	B
Pvt. Jesse Baldridge	30	B
Pvt. Jesse Baldridge	23	K
Pvt. Ned Baldridge	21	C
Pvt. Samuel Baldridge	25	K
Pvt. Weetiney Baldridge	24	B
Bugler Wilson Baldridge	19	B
Pvt. Jeff Ballow	26	I
Pvt. David Barbara (Barbery)	26	C
Pvt. Bark	40	C
Pvt. Frank Bat	25	A
Sgt. Bat Puppy	48	K
Pvt. Arch Beamer	20	D
Pvt. West Beamer	40	H
Pvt. Charles Bean	19	H
Lt. John Bear Meat	39	I
Pvt. Packen ham Bear meat	47	I
Pvt. Bear Paw	49	C
Bugler Bear Paw	24	G

Name	Age	Company
Pvt. Cornelius Bear Sitting Down	30	G
Pvt. Hicory Beaver	24	K
Pvt. Lewis Beaver	30	K
Pvt. Jim Beavertail	33	H
Pvt. Beaver toater ah le chel	29	G
Pvt. John Beeff	22	McD
Pvt. Samuel Bell	26	McD
Pvt. Alex Ben	20	K
Pvt. Bend About	25	E
Lt. Anderson Benge	41	A
Lt. George Benge	26	K
Pvt. John Benge	18	F
Pvt. Ned Benge	19	H
Capt. Pickens M. Benge	32	K
Pvt. Richard Benge	19	K
Pvt. Big Arch	50	I
Pvt. Big Bullett	35	E
Pvt. Big Feather Chu wa loo kee	26	I
Pvt. Arch Bigfoot	33	E
Pvt. Daniel Big Head	30	I
Pvt. Jack Big	50	A
Pvt. Joseph Bigjack	25	A
Pvt. Big Road	30	D
Pvt. Big Sides	70	H
Lt. Big sky yah too kah	33	McD
Cpl. Bird	35	E
Sgt. Bird	40	K
Pvt. Baldridge Bird	30	G
Pvt. Grapes Bird	20	K
Pvt. Sanders Bird	19	H
Pvt. Bird Chopper	29	A
Bugler Bird Chopper	23	E
Pvt. James Birdtail	30	C
Pvt. Little Terapin Black	18	G
Pvt. James Blackcoat	42	F
Smith Ezekiel Blackfox	28	G
Pvt. Henry Black Fox	20	A
Pvt. Black Haw	30	A

Name	Age	Company
Pvt. Black Haw	32	D
Pvt. Black Haw	32	E
Pvt. Pettet Black Haw	26	B
Pvt. Black Haw Crawfish	26	I
Pvt. Blacksmith	27	I
Pvt. Lewis Blair	23	K
Pvt. George Blanket	20	H
Pvt. Proctor Blue	20	E
Pvt. Luke Bluebird	22	H
Sgt. George Boar	55	I
Pvt. Jack Board	27	B
Sgt. John Boggs	40	B
Pvt. Shoe boots Boggs	22	B
Pvt. Buck Boling	30	F
Pvt. Bottle	19	B
Pvt. Joseph Bottle	26	I
Pvt. Judge Bottle	29	I
Pvt. James Bowen	19	E
Pvt. Dick Bowles	23	I
Pvt. Tah lar lor Bowles	40	I
Pvt. James Bowls	26	C
Pvt. John Bowls	21	C
Pvt. Johnson Bowls	21	C
Pvt. Bread Oo nur we ya lie	60	E
Pvt. Jesse Brewer	60	A
Pvt. Thomas Brewer	40	C
Pvt. Christy Broad	18	K
Cpl. Broom	39	E
Pvt. Arch Broom	29	F
Pvt. Bear Broom	25	F
Pvt. Richard Broom	25	F
Pvt. Bill Brown	18	K
Pvt. George Brush	26	F
Pvt. John Buck	30	A
Sgt. Jess Buckskin	40	A
Bugler Buffalo	25	C
Pvt. Bull	52	C
Pvt. Bullfrog	18	H

Name	Age	Company
Pvt. Dave Bull Frog	30	D
Pvt. George Bullfrog	20	F
Pvt. Moses Bullfrog	42	F
Discharged, unfit, 11/12/1861		
Pvt. Robin Bull Frog	42	C
Pvt. Bull Frog koo weeskoo wie	19	I
Pvt. Wilson Bull Frog	29	G
Pvt. Bill Bump	26	K
Pvt. Bunch ne cow ie	20	E
Pvt. Bunch Rabbit	18	E
Pvt. John Burgess	20	C
Pvt. Daniel Burntwood	32	F
Farrier Henry Bushyhead	47	G
Pvt. George Butler	23	F
Pvt. William Cade	24	H
Pvt. Cah le ger	29	K
Pvt. Cah lie skai wee	22	G
Cpl. Cah lor nu hay ske	59	B
Pvt. Pa sooz or kie Cah lor nu hay skie	28	B
Pvt. Tro loh tay nute Cah lor nu hay skie	30	B
Pvt. Johe Cah nay soo lay skie	36	I
Sgt. Cah no hay tat at quah	35	I
Pvt. Cah quah ter or Havy	22	D
Pvt. Cah sar he la	46	McD
Pvt. Dick Cah see lowie	19	I
Pvt. Ezekiel Cah see lowie	21	I
Sgt. Proctor Cah se lah wie	37	McD
Pvt. Cah Soo yoh Kie Gritts	25	C
Pvt. Cah tah yae tah	22	H
Pvt. Cah tur tah tu Terrapin	56	B
Cpl. Cal le tol ter	40	C
Pvt. Jack Camrol	20	A
Pvt. Budman Canoo	40	C
Asst. Surgeon Joseph W. Carden	35	Staff
Resigned 4/7/1862		
Pvt. Car nos gah	22	F
Pvt. Car Sah tah	23	H
Pvt. Car ter oot Sun nah	20	H

Name	Age	Company
Pvt. Carter oo yor lor choo he	20	H
Pvt. Moses Catchem	35	I
Pvt. Ben Catcher	25	I
Cpl. Ellis Catcher	28	I
Pvt. Man Killer Catcher	34	B
Pvt. Jack Catfish	25	H
Pvt. Cay noo qee kee ner	36	I
Pvt. Chah yah nur Doochis tah	70	G
Pvt. Cha loo ky	25	A
Pvt. Walker Chambers	35	F
Farrier William Chambers	44	E
Pvt. Charles	18	McD
Pvt. Dick Charles	24	G
Pvt. Char ne way noh wily	35	B
Pvt. Chee lo ter ta Ky	31	D
Pvt. Chee Stay cha	25	B
Pvt. Chee stoo/Rabbit	20	H
Cpl. Chee wah Stah taw	32	F
Che lah che lah	—	F
Name canceled		
Pvt. Che lah Ke te hee	35	F
Pvt. Che nah que	45	B
Pvt. Che ne que	57	C
Pvt. Che quah Kiel	20	E
Pvt. Che Squy ah Weaver	24	B
Pvt. Bill Chewa looky	23	McD
Pvt. Chewie	24	McD
Pvt. Lewis Chicken	29	F
Pvt. Samuel Chicken	22	F
Pvt. Chicken Cock	22	D
Pvt. Rider Chicken	20	A
Lt. Christy (Christie) Chicken toater	40	E
Farrier Daniel Childers	26	McD
Pvt. Napoleon Childers	21	McD
Pvt. Robert P. Childers	33	McD
Pvt. Chillee	25	F
Pvt. John Chocktaw	46	C
Pvt. Thompson Choo Kah la ter	40	E

Name	Age	Company
Pvt. Choo ke yah skie	25	E
Pvt. Tom Choo le Stee	22	H
Pvt. Ned Chool Squah loo tah	28	I
Pvt. Chool Squa loo tah White Bird	52	I
Pvt. Choo noo lur hus ky	30	E
Pvt. Choon stoo tee cha nay wo tay ski	50	B
Pvt. Sequoyah Choon Stortie	18	I
Pvt. Cho wail cer	24	I
Pvt. Allan Christie	40	A
Smith Watt Christie (Christy)	41	E
Pvt. Arch Christy	30	E
Pvt. Dick Christy	27	B
Pvt. James Christy	20	E
Pvt. Chu caw mer der	21	F
Pvt. Chu Chu	40	B
Pvt. Moses Chu glater	30	K
Pvt. Joseph Chu he tler	25	A
Pvt. George Chu le oh wie	70	E
Pvt. Chu lis quit ty	30	I
Pvt. Chu lix Sie	21	E
Pvt. Chu loe csgee Wolf	35	G
Pvt. Chu lu ya skie	22	E
Cpl. Chu nog hur kee	31	I
Pvt. Chu nu lis ke	20	G
Pvt. Chu stoo lu	25	E
Pvt. Chu wae lu kee	40	H
Pvt. Dave Chu wa loo ke	20	D
Pvt. Chu Wee	24	A
Lt. Joseph Chu wee	35	G
Pvt. Chu we skah Ah dah ke to hee	22	G
Pvt. Chu wo yee	55	G
Pvt. Chu yah skil kee	40	F
Pvt. Henry Clay	32	B
Pvt. Samuel Cloud	29	B
Pvt. Coffee	40	G
Pvt. John Coldman	28	C
Pvt. Cold Weather	18	D
Pvt. Jack Cold Weather	35	B

Name	Age	Company
Pvt. Bat Colston	25	D
Pvt. Daniel Colston	20	B
Pvt. Sam Colston	22	McD
Pvt. William Colston	40	C
Pvt. Columbus	18	K
Pvt. Coming Deer	45	H
Pvt. Peter Coming Deer	19	K
Pvt. Nick Coolah chie	34	D
Pvt. Coo los tah	32	F
Pvt. Coon	35	F
Pvt. Daniel Cornass	25	B
Pvt. Dick Corn Silk	47	G
Pvt. Joseph Cornsilk	50	F
Later a lieutenant		
Pvt. Thomas Cornsilk	35	F
Pvt. Spirit Cornsilk	23	D
Pvt. Corn Tassel	32	D
Pvt. Crawfish	23	D
Sgt. Robert Crawford	34	F
Pvt. Crawler	40	E
Pvt. Crawler Proctor	18	K
Pvt. Crawling Dick	20	E
Pvt. Clark Crawling snake	30	D
Pvt. Arch Creek	18	B
Pvt. George Creek	30	B
Pvt. Jim Creek	30	B
Pvt. Creek Billy	36	F
Pvt. Creek Charles	20	K
Pvt. Creek David	30	K
Pvt. Creek Jim	40	K
Pvt. Creek Samuel	20	K
Pvt. Andrew Crittendon	30	G
Pvt. Crying Bear	24	A
Pvt. Crying Bear	36	I
Pvt. David Cryingbird	19	F
Pvt. Crying Wolfe	40	D
Pvt. Cul ca yer Smith	29	A
Pvt. Cul cur los kee	55	H

Name	Age	Company
Pvt. Cul kah los kee	30	B
Pvt. Cul stu him sky	66	D
Pvt. Cur tee suttee Oo tah nee yar tah	30	I
Pvt. Cut his head off	22	C
Pvt. Daniel	18	E
Pvt. Darke	55	F
Pvt. David Daugherty	26	H
Sgt. John Daugherty	32	G
Pvt. Davidson	30	A
Pvt. Davis	20	D
Pvt. John Davis	30	D
Capt. John Porum Davis	38	C
Pvt. Dee gee mee	18	F
Pvt. James Deer Head	46	B
Pvt. John Deerhead	30	F
Pvt. Deer in the Water	22	K
Lt. Josiah Deer in the Water	—	B
Pvt. Deer in the water Tah che hoo stah	28	B
Pvt. Watt Dew	25	F
Pvt. Henry Dick	22	H
Pvt. Isaac Dick	50	D
Pvt. Richard Dick	25	B
Pvt. Dirt Hunter	20	C
Pvt. Dirt Eater	18	A
Pvt. Dirt eater Ah cor tay skie	21	I
Pvt. Dirt Eater Beg mush	36	I
Pvt. Dirt Pott	23	McD
Pvt. Dirt Thrower	30	K
Pvt. Harris Diver	44	E
Pvt. Moses Dog in the Bush	30	B
Pvt. Jesse Dogwood	34	McD
Pvt. Joseph Dogwood	30	E
Pvt. Alex Dollar	25	E
Pvt. No name Dollars	—	E
Pvt. Che neh que Dorchester	40	B
Pvt. George Downing	22	I
Pvt. Johnson Downing	27	I
Chaplain Lewis Downing	38	Staff

Name	Age	Company
Pvt. Mink Downing	38	K
Lt. Samuel Downing	19	H
Pvt. Jesse Draging	22	E
Pvt. Draging Canoe	30	E
Pvt. Dreadful Water	31	H
Pvt. George Dreadful Water	20	McD
Lt. Charles Drew	38	C
Colonel John Drew	65	Staff
Pvt. Drinker	—	E
Pvt. Driving out	28	K
Pvt. Dropper	30	F
Lt. Noah Drowning Bear	28	McD
Pvt. Drumfish (Creek)	30	K
Pvt. Drunk	20	C
Pvt. Dry Peter	30	G
Pvt. Dry Squirrel	32	G
Pvt. Dry Water	35	C
Pvt. Dave Duck	25	A
Pvt. Dick Duck	22	McD
Pvt. John Duck	26	E
Pvt. Stephen Duck	19	McD
Pvt. David Duvall	23	F
Pvt. Rogers Duvall	35	F
Pvt. E char chy	22	D
Pvt. Wolf E coo wee	26	D
Pvt. E cow ee Kah von Keely	25	D
Pvt. Ee tah Kur Stah Sequayah	19	I
Pvt. E lah we	50	F
Cpl. James Ellis	35	K
Pvt. Peter Ellis	24	K
Cpl. Samuel Ellis	30	K
Bugler William Ellis	18	K
Pvt. Elno la Kay no Sos Ky	22	D
Pvt. E low ie	34	A
Pvt. E low ie	30	D
Pvt. Elow ie Oo te ter a hie	47	I
Pvt. Ely Ah nee tah Kay yah	33	I
Pvt. Peter Emory	35	F

Name	Age	Company
Pvt. Joseph England	21	D
Pvt. E nor la Te Kus Key	22	D
Pvt. E nov le	19	H
Pvt. E noy le skon nah dah hee	33	G
Pvt. E tan tes skie	38	E
Surgeon James P. Evans	55	Staff
Captured at Pea Ridge		
Hospital Steward Pvt. Walter N. Evans	18	H
Captured at Pea Ridge		
Sgt. John Even	30	C
Pvt. Ever Sought	25	K
Pvt. Falling	28	McD
Pvt. Dick Falling	22	McD
Pvt. Jesse Falling	34	A
Farrier Falling Pot	40	A
Pvt. Fawn Head	40	K
Cpl. Fawn Killer	27	C
Pvt. Watt Fielding	34	G
Pvt. Daniel Fields	31	F
Capt. Richard Fields	59	F
Captured at Pea Ridge		
Pvt. Thomas Fields	21	F
Pvt. Wiley Fields	26	D
Pvt. Fire throun Henderson	35	E
Pvt. John Fish	55	F
Smith Levi Fish	33	McD
Lt. Nathaniel (Nathan) Fish	54	H
Pvt. John Flute	18	B
Sgt. Flute Fox Skin	45	B
Cpl. Flying Bird	30	McD
Pvt. Flying nun dah ee	35	G
Lt. Fogg	47	E
Pvt. Alexander Foreman	25	C
Pvt. Arch Foreman	18	D
Pvt. George Foreman	19	H
Lt. Samuel Foster	42	I
Bugler Jack Fox	32	A
Pvt. Fox Mouse	27	A

Name	Age	Company
Pvt. Screech Owl Fox	26	K
Cpl. French	35	H
Sgt. Frog	60	A
Pvt. Tee Sas Kie Frog	44	E
Pvt. Jesse Frog Jaw	31	McD
Pvt. Gah dah oo ne gah hah nah	16	F
Pvt. Archilla Gee Sur woh Yee	30	McD
Pvt. Tom Girl Catcher	25	McD
Pvt. Watt Girth	25	D
Pvt. Judge Glass	19	C
Pvt. Dick Glory	30	E
Pvt. Moses Glory	32	McD
Pvt. Gnat	50	McD
Cpl. Go-back	38	H
Pvt. Jack Gobbler	35	McD
Pvt. Lewis Going Back	25	McD
Pvt. Going Snake	19	E
Pvt. Gone in the Water	25	F
Pvt. Good Money	32	K
Pvt. Johnson Good Money	25	I
Pvt. Grapes	25	McD
Pvt. Oo wa loo Kee Graves	37	C
Bugler George Grease	18	H
Pvt. Greece	28	C
Smith William Green	37	F
Pvt. Jack Griffin	33	C
Pvt. Joseph Griffin	26	C
Pvt. Grimmitt	33	E
Pvt. William Grits	30	H
Cpl. Gritts	60	McD
Pvt. Jim Gritts	18	McD
Pvt. Westly Gritts	35	H
Pvt. Nelson Grubbs	22	I
Farrier George Guess	26	C
Cpl. Ned Gunpile	40	F
Pvt. Robert Gunrod	16	McD
Sgt. John Hair	37	H
Sgt. Wilson Hair	30	B

Name	Age	Company
Pvt. Samuel Halcomb	28	K
Pvt. Hammer	22	K
Cpl. James Hammer	36	C
Pvt. John Hammer	33	McD
Sgt. Dempsey Handle	27	F
Pvt. Ha ne	22	F
Pvt. Hanging Honey Oo che skie lah	50	B
Pvt. Thomas Harnage	20	B
Pvt. William Harris	39	C
Pvt. Jacob Hatchett	29	H
Pvt. John Hatchett	30	H
Pvt. Tom Hatchett	25	H
Sgt. Alex Hawk	26	McD
Pvt. Dick Hawk	16	H
Pvt. John Hawk	22	H
Pvt. Lacey Hawkins	30	I
Pvt. Lewis Hawk	35	I
Pvt. Hawk Nettle carrier	30	E
Lt. Lacy Hawkins	30	A
Pvt. Heavy	30	D
Sgt. Willie Hendricks	27	H
Pvt. Arch Henry	29	G
Lt. Jesse Henry	35	G
Pvt. Thomas Henry	27	C
Pvt. He Sar tas Kee	23	D
Sgt. William Hewbanks	21	H
Pvt. Crawler Hicks	35	F
Capt. Edward R. Hicks	29	H
Capt. Jefferson D. Hicks	35	A
Pvt. Hiding Man te cab ne ye skie	30	G
Capt. Isaac N. Hildebrand	39	D
Pvt. Joseph Hildebrand	24	A
Pvt. George Hogg	56	I
Pvt. Hogshooter	30	A
Pvt. Nelson Hogshooter	18	D
Pvt. Jim Hogskin	30	A
Pvt. Hogtoter	54	E
Pvt. Sunday Hogtoter	20	E

Name	Age	Company
Pvt. David Holmes	20	K
Pvt. Ely Holt	28	K
Pvt. Barrow Hood	32	K
Pvt. Daniel G. Hoppe	50	B
Pvt. Thompson Horn	35	F
Pvt. William Horn	19	H
Pvt. Watt Horsefly	21	D
Pvt. Jackson Housebig	27	G
Pvt. Houston	27	I
Pvt. Humming Bird	20	F
Pvt. Cloy See Nah Hummingbird	30	B
Pvt. Watt Hummingbird	21	K
Pvt. Hungry	42	McD
Pvt. Jack Ice	28	B
Pvt. John Ice	20	H
Pvt. Isaac	35	A
Pvt. Isaac	30	D
Pvt. Isaac	23	E
Pvt. Philip Israel	20	H
Pvt. Is Sar gur/Breather	36	K
Pvt. Jack oo sa nah lee	31	E
Pvt. Jack Rabbit	35	G
Pvt. Jackson	35	C
Sgt. Jackson	38	K
Pvt. Walter Jackson	20	C
Pvt. Wily Jackson	19	C
Pvt. James	19	D
Pvt. Dutchy James	18	B
Sgt. Mill James	29	McD
Pvt. Jesse (a Creek)	30	F
Pvt. Adam John	25	I
Pvt. Johnson	30	A
Pvt. Alex Johnson	18	E
Pvt. Jack Johnson	23	C
Pvt. Jack Johnson	—	D
Sgt. Josiah	40	A
Pvt. Josiah	22	D
Pvt. Jass ee	35	K

Name	Age	Company
Pvt. Jue wayne Dah gur doh see	46	G
Pvt. Jumpe Creek	35	B
Pvt. Jumper	23	H
Pvt. Jumper	20	K
Pvt. Jack Jumper	19	C
Sgt. Mills Jumper	27	McD
Pvt. Stitch Jumper	19	C
Pvt. Stephen Kah mer Se tay ski	25	B
Pvt. Kah Nah le la	30	A
Pvt. Kah Now Sos Kee	30	D
Pvt. Kah nuch chie	23	E
Pvt. Kah Se lah w'e	30	E
Sgt. Kas Knu ne Man Killer	38	E
Pvt. Kay noo gee Rising Fawn	22	I
Pvt. Kay Skene ny	25	McD
Pvt. Kee loh Ste	20	D
Pvt. Daniel Keenah	19	I
Pvt. Kee nah Tu Kah	26	C
Pvt. Joe Keener	40	I
Pvt. Ned Kee ner	37	D
Pvt. Aaron Ke lar ne gah	27	G
Pvt. Ker lur Soo Kee sky	30	A
Pvt. Ker na Soo tie	36	A
Pvt. Ker ne too	40	A
Comm. Frederick A. Kerr	49	Staff
Dropped August 2, 1862		
Pvt. Ketchum	44	D
Pvt. Ketchum too nie	38	F
Pvt. Kick up Punkin Pile	40	I
Pvt. Archy Kiley	30	A
Pvt. Sam Kill ah ne gah	20	K
Pvt. Arch E. Kills	36	G
Pvt. William King Fisher	28	I
Pvt. Koo wee skoo wee	45	I
Pvt. John Koo wee skoo wee	17	I
Pvt. George Koo we skoo we	25	H
Pvt. Moses Kuh lee Skuy wie	24	B
Pvt. Joseph Kuh lee skuy wiee	24	B

Name	Age	Company
Pvt. Kur la nes Ky	22	A
Pvt. Kur lee tah Coon	27	I
Pvt. Lacey	36	McD
Pvt. Martin Langy	23	C
Cpl. John Larchy	60	D
Pvt. John Larchy Che nahque	32	I
Pvt. Lar Kin ee	22	I
Pvt. Lawrie	42	E
Cpl. Leach	37	B
Pvt. Leaf	45	McD
Pvt. James Lee	40	K
Pvt. Left Hand	16	McD
Pvt. Le to wade	33	F
Pvt. Lewis	28	K
Cpl. Little Allen	20	K
Pvt. Bird Little	23	G
Pvt. Little Bird	48	McD
Pvt. William Little Bird	25	B
Pvt. Little Dae	30	A
Pvt. Little Deer	21	H
Pvt. Little Dick	32	McD
Pvt. Little Girl	30	McD
Pvt. Little hair Big mush	35	I
Pvt. Little Jess	30	C
Pvt. Little Jesse	43	H
Pvt. Little Jim	55	McD
Pvt. Little Peter	55	A
Lt. Little Red/Redbird/Little Bird	41	I
Pvt. Lizzard	32	C
Pvt. Rider Lizzard	38	F
Discharged unfit 11/12/61		
Pvt. John Long	23	H
Pvt. Allen Long	30	K
Pvt. Alex Love	33	D
Pvt. Johnson Love	30	C
Pvt. Low Cat	30	F
Pvt. John Lowry	26	F
Pvt. Lying Fish Dai gur gah	40	G

Name	Age	Company
Pvt. Cherokee Manning	33	H
Pvt. Lah chee Manning	20	I
Pvt. Ah lee che Martin	32	B
Pvt. Jackson Martin	25	B
Pvt. Jackson Martin	20	B
Pvt. John Matier	25	H
Pvt. Richard Matlear	22	K
Pvt. Robin Matoy	37	C
Pvt. Mawking Crows	30	McD
Pvt. Reynolds May	—	—
Prisoner, Discharged hospital, 10/30/1862		
Cpl. Creek McCoy	40	F
Pvt. Thomas McCoy	23	F
Capt. James McDaniel	43	McD
Pvt. Dave McKinsie	40	McD
Pvt. Jack McKinsie	18	McD
Pvt. McLamore	24	H
Pvt. Looney McLane (McLain)	18	B
Pvt. Thomas Meat	20	C
Pvt. Henry Meigs	20	H
Pvt. Messenger	21	G
Pvt. Roly Middlestriker	25	K
Pvt. Andrew Miller	16	A
Pvt. George Mills	19	McD
Sgt. William Mills	37	F
Pvt. Mink	26	C
Pvt. Mister Billy	30	F
Pvt. Ned Mole	35	K
Pvt. Money Crier	27	K
Pvt. James Money Crier	33	F
Pvt. Money Hunter	34	I
Cpl. Moses	30	D
Pvt. Moses	22	E
Pvt. Moses	18	H
Pvt. George Moses	23	E
Pvt. Jack Moses	23	G
Pvt. Adam Mouse	18	A
Not mustered in, AWOL		

Name	Age	Company
Pvt. Comings Murphy	28	McD
Cpl. Saturday Murphy	30	H
Pvt. Tee cah toh skie Murphy	50	B
Pvt. Mush	38	C
Pvt. Henry Mush	30	I
Pvt. Lewis Mush	26	E
Pvt. William Mush Rat	18	E
Pvt. Musk Mellon	19	K
Pvt. Johnson Muskrat	48	G
Bugler John Myers	22	McD
Pvt. Nah che ah	25	McD
Pvt. Nah hoo lar	24	A
Pvt. Nah yoo take / Rock Thrower	38	C
Pvt. John Jacob Ned	20	G
Pvt. Nedson	30	K
Pvt. Ben Nedson	20	K
Pvt. Ne ler ca yer	22	A
Pvt. Nelson	26	F
Pvt. Ned Nettle carra	26	E
Pvt. Nick	38	A
Pvt. Nick	30	F
Pvt. Noisy Dah ske ke de he	20	G
Pvt. Noisy Water Nick	39	B
Pvt. Andrew No Wife	22	B
Pvt. Oak Ball	58	G
Pvt. Ned Oakball	20	G
Pvt. Oh tah nah ees ky Nur yan ka han	20	I
Pvt. Old Buffalo	17	C
Pvt. Old Horse	45	A
Pvt. Old Rabbit	59	McD
Pvt. Oo chee Tee hee	26	I
Pvt. Oo che loe tie / Oochalata / Charles Thompson	30	A
Pvt. Davis Oo hah loo ke	35	D
Pvt. Oo har lu ge	48	G
Pvt. Oo her loo ky	54	D
Pvt. Oo kah hah ter	22	A
Pvt. Oo kee lah ny	20	I

Name	Age	Company
Pvt. Oo kees quaw ter	51	A
Pvt. Oo Kil e Soo	30	I
Pvt. Ook tay rie Wolf	22	I
Pvt. Ool ah hey at Corn Silk	30	K
Pvt. Oo lan So ner	55	E
Pvt. Oo la Whatee	30	A
Pvt. Oo lee stoo Stephen	18	G
Pvt. Oo le stoo wah lah whe dah	20	G
Pvt. Ool le now ee	65	D
Pvt. Oo lho nah ste skie noo chah we	20	G
Pvt. Oo lor nah stee skie	18	K
Pvt. Ool Skun nie	20	C
Pvt. Oo luy hee yah tah Tah nee moh tey se	22	B
Pvt. Oon Clau e sur	23	H
Pvt. Lucy Oo nay cur sen	20	B
Pvt. Oo ne che chu Kestie	48	I
Pvt. Oo ner chos ty	35	A
Pvt. Oo ne tler	40	A
Pvt. Oo no la te ka lee sky	32	A
Pvt. Ben Oo war nun kee	27	H
Pvt. Oo Skur tur ne chy	30	E
Pvt. Oo Squah loo gah	47	E
Pvt. Joseph Oo Stil hy	19	K
Pvt. Oowa loo kee	28	C
Pvt. Oo tah he tah	20	F
Cpl. Oo tah ne yau cah	55	McD
Pvt. Ootah ne yunter	47	D
Cpl. Oo tah tay gee skee	34	I
Pvt. Oo tar tlor hee ter	25	D
Pvt. Oo tchay lur nur Sequoyah	19	I
Pvt. Oo te sah tah	35	H
Pvt. Dave Oote Sah tuh	17	H
Pvt. Oo tla noh tuer	30	E
Pvt. Moses Oo tuttie	20	H
Pvt. Oo wah kah Lewis	18	I
Pvt. Oo wah wor See ty	40	D
Pvt. John Oo wa lo kee	20	C
Pvt. Oo wa loo kie Bighead	50	C

Name	Age	Company
Pvt. Samuel Wal tay	19	B
Pvt. Oo war lay skie	30	I
Pvt. George Oo war nun ke	19	H
Pvt. Oo way te	18	D
Pvt. Oo wa yer Sut tie	30	I
Pvt. Oo wor ser tie Skelley	25	I
Pvt. Oo yor se stah che yah tee hah	25	B
Pvt. Oo yor ter	35	A
Pvt. Or cha gee sky	20	E
Pvt. Samuel Osage	24	B
Pvt. Judge Otter	20	F
Pvt. Ottor	22	C
Pvt. Dave Packenham	19	A
Pvt. Tom Packing	23	I
Pvt. John Panther	22	D
Pvt. Parch Meal	60	I
Farrier Path Killer	56	B
Pvt. Path Killer	22	K
Pvt. Path Killer	52	McD
Pvt. James Patrick	22	H
Pvt. George Peach Eater	45	E
Pvt. John Peacheater	30	K
Pvt. Robert Peel	21	McD
Major Thomas Pegg	53	Staff
Sgt. Peter	27	H
Pvt. William Peter	18	McD
Pvt. Levy Pettit	23	K
Pvt. Pheasant	60	McD
Pvt. Picket	17	F
Pvt. Pick up Money	29	McD
Pvt. Jim Piddy	36	C
Captured at Pea Ridge, died 3/30/1862		
Pvt. John Pig	29	McD
Pvt. Pigeon	25	McD
Pvt. Josiah Pigeon	33	E
Capt. Albert Pike	30	I
Pvt. Poo Bear	30	B
Pvt. Eli Poor Boy	27	B

Name	Age	Company
Pvt. Samuel Poor Boy	25	B
Pvt. Davissy Porham	17	C
Pvt. Post Silk	20	K
Pvt. Thomas Potatoe	35	McD
Pvt. Pot Kicker	21	McD
Pvt. Ely Pott	19	K
Pvt. George Pott	20	F
Pvt. Thomas Pott	25	D
Pvt. John Pottatoe	19	McD
Pvt. Isaac Potts	38	B
Pvt. Charles Pouch	43	I
Cpl. Powel	40	D
Cpl. Um ah hoo gee Pritchet	60	G
Pvt. George Pritchett	30	B
Pvt. Jack Pritchett	40	E
Pvt. John Pritchett	19	E
Pvt. Mike Pritchett	35	H
Pvt. Adam Proctor	25	G
Pvt. Arch Proctor	22	G
Pvt. Drinking Proctor	20	K
Pvt. Isaac Proctor	19	K
Pvt. John Proctor	26	E
Sgt. Johnson Proctor	35	G
Pvt. Joseph Proctor	18	E
Pvt. Peter Proctor	20	K
Pvt. Ben Pumpkin	18	A
Pvt. Charlie Pumpkin	17	G
Pvt. Jesse Pumpkin	23	D
Pvt. Moses Punkin Pile	24	I
Pvt. William Punkin pile	22	I
Pvt. Queen	20	H
Pvt. Daniel Quinton	20	K
Pvt. Lewis Quinton	22	K
Pvt. Andrew Rabbit	24	E
Pvt. Rafter Jaybird	30	H
Pvt. Arch Raincrow	23	H
Pvt. Jim Raincrow	22	H
Pvt. Tony Raincrow	39	F

Name	Age	Company
Pvt. David Rat	46	F
Pvt. John Rat	25	G
Pvt. Richard Ratcliff	26	C
Pvt. John Ratcliffe	16	B
Pvt. Ratling Goard Rider	24	D
Pvt. Red Bird	25	C
Pvt. Red Bird	30	F
Pvt. Red Bird	21	G
Pvt. Daniel Red Bird	30	A
Pvt. Jack Redbird	29	G
Pvt. Jesse Redbird	27	G
Pvt. Ridge	22	K
Pvt. John Ridge	37	F
Pvt. John Ridge	25	G
Pvt. Ridge chu we skah	30	G
Pvt. John Riley	28	B
Pvt. Samuel Riley	36	B
Pvt. Robber	28	F
Pvt. Robin	30	H
Pvt. Richard Robinson	16	H
Pvt. David Roeoe	40	A
Pvt. Rogers	40	D
Cpl. Alexander Rogers	23	C
Sgt. John Rogers	40	A
Bugler John Rogers	30	H
Pvt. Lovely Rogers	21	F
Farrier Rogers Silk	28	K
Pvt. Rope Camroe	47	A
Pvt. Rosin	30	F
Sgt. Allen Ross	44	H
Son of Chief Ross		
Lt. George Washington Ross	30	H
Son of Chief Ross		
Pvt. Jonah J. Ross	23	G
Pvt. Oliver Ross	40	K
Sgt. Thomas Ross	38	K
Lt. Col. William Potter Ross	41	Staff
Pvt. Major Round	22	F

Name	Age	Company
Pvt. Rounder	45	D
Pvt. French Rowe	30	E
Pvt. Jack Rowe	17	C
Pvt. Levi Rowe	37	E
Pvt. Runabout	20	A
Pvt. Runabout	22	F
Pvt. Runabout	21	H
Lt. Samuel Runaway	35	D
Pvt. Runaway Person	20	D
Pvt. Chekele Runner	45	G
Lt. Ezekiel Russell	39	D
Pvt. S. Ney	35	McD
Pvt. Sah Nah Ne	30	K
Pvt. Sah ne Te Kin Nie	30	E
Pvt. Salt	55	F
Pvt. Jack Sam	23	McD
Pvt. Samuel	30	F
Pvt. Dave Sanders	18	B
Lt. George O. Sanders	24	B
Pvt. James Sanders	20	H
Pvt. John Sanders	29	C
Pvt. John G. Sanders	20	C
Pvt. Joseph Sanders	40	I
Pvt. Mitchell Sanders	22	G
Capt. Nicholas B. Sanders	43	B
Pvt. Sar Ke Yah Sanders	20	H
Pvt. Sap Sucker	25	K
Pvt. Sau ny	26	D
Pvt. Bill Sca lol le	20	McD
Sgt. Edward Scorn	29	E
Pvt. Alex Scott	42	E
Pvt. Edward Scott	32	E
Pvt. Harry Scott	40	I
Pvt. Scraper	35	F
Lt. Arch (Archibald) Scraper	36	G
Pvt. Buck Scraper	21	C
Capt. George W. Scraper	43	G
Cpl. Henry H. Scraper	20	G

Name	Age	Company
Pvt. John Scraper	25	F
Cpl. Otter Scraper	26	G
Sgt. William Scraper	22	G
Pvt. Scud dis	40	I
Sgt. John Sebolt	28	K
Pvt. Seckeomey Tee cahlor hay Nah	22	I
Pvt. Charles Se cow ie	19	A
Pvt. See cah we	32	G
Cpl. Seed Catcher	49	B
Pvt. Se que ah	28	K
Pvt. Sequoyah	19	D
Sgt. George Seven	40	D
Sgt. Bushyhead Sevier	30	C
Sgt. Shell	38	G
Pvt. Jesse Shell	22	G
Pvt. Jack She Rain	19	K
Pvt. Sherain Leap	25	G
Pvt. Ned Short Arrow	42	B
Pvt. Arch Simmons	60	F
Pvt. Jess Simmons	24	C
Pvt. Watt Simmons	20	F
Pvt. William Simmons	20	C
Pvt. Wilson Simmons	30	F
Pvt. Simon	16	McD
Pvt. Sit noo wa Kie	60	E
Pvt. Sitting bare Fishing Hawk	39	G
Pvt. Tom Sittingdown	33	I
Pvt. Wilson Sittingdown	24	K
Pvt. Sitting on Bridge	50	D
Pvt. Johnson Sit w wa Ky	21	A
Pvt. Six	40	A
Pvt. Co ley Six Killer	28	K
Pvt. Humming bird Six Killer	30	I
Pvt. Six killr ski ya too ka	30	E
Pvt. Allen Skahlol	32	McD
Pvt. Skah yah too gah Sahle goo war	35	G
Pvt. Tom Ska lol	28	McD
Smith Sker Kee my	40	D

Name	Age	Company
Pvt. Skilp	40	C
Pvt. Lewis Skon tah hee	27	B
Pvt. Moses Skon tah hee	40	B
Pvt. Wiley Slop	33	D
Pvt. Small Dirt	36	C
Pvt. Small Dirt	28	K
Lt. Crab Grass Smith	32	K
Lt. Eli Smith	54	E
Sgt. George Smith	28	E
Pvt. Isaac Smith	27	A
Sgt. Jesse Smith	30	D
Pvt. John Smith	40	F
Lt. Samuel H. Smith	40	C
Pvt. Smith Tah chai Kes	22	C
Pvt. John Smoke	30	G
Pvt. Smoker Gordon	19	C
Pvt. Slarch (Arch) Snail	21	D
Killed by Watie's men		
Pvt. Simon Snail	24	D
Pvt. Track Snake	21	D
Pvt. Aaron Soap	21	E
Pvt. John Soap	28	I
Pvt. Soap Kan noo le Skee	30	G
Pvt. Soap Nich	24	E
Pvt. Soap oo yah skah wo tie	42	G
Pvt. Soap Toy oo nese	23	G
Pvt. James Soldirr	26	K
Pvt. Soldum	26	F
Pvt. John Something	26	McD
Pvt. Soo Chy	30	A
Pvt. Soo Wa Ky	30	D
Pvt. William Sour John	46	I
Pvt. Davis Spaniard	30	G
Pvt. Arch Spears	26	A
Pvt. Bird Spears	45	F
Pvt. Stephen Spears	21	B
Pvt. Wilson Spears	28	F
Pvt. Alick Spike/Treasurer	32	D

Name	Age	Company
Pvt. Ned Spiller	35	D
Pvt. Spirit	48	A
Pvt. Spirit	37	F
Pvt. Spirit	28	K
Pvt. Spirit Sam	18	I
Lt. George Springston	22	D
Pvt. Spring Water	25	K
Pvt. Spunk	76	A
Pvt. Squah Ne char	48	G
Pvt. Squah ta le chy	30	A
Pvt. John Sauirel (Squirrel)	20	A
Died of disease, 11/22/1861		
Pvt. Squirrel	25	C
Pvt. Squirrel	25	D
Pvt. Samuel Squirrel	20	F
Pvt. Watt Squirrel	30	G
Pvt. Squirrel Chicken	20	F
Sgt. Stagger	38	I
Pvt. Arch Stand	31	E
Pvt. Standing Buck	41	McD
Lt. Deer in the Water Star	43	C
Pvt. Ezekiel Starr	22	C
Pvt. John Starr	23	D
Pvt. Squirrel Starr	23	C
Pvt. Whitekiller Starr	22	E
Pvt. Steelum	25	D
Pvt. Stee ny Soo Wah tee	20	D
Pvt. Ste he Kee	51	G
Pvt. Stephen	22	G
Cpl. Cook Still	29	E
Pvt. Josiah Still	27	C
Pvt. Charley Stinson	20	McD
Pvt. William Stinson	23	McD
Lt. Watt Stop	42	McD
Cpl. Charles Stople	50	F
Pvt. Stop skon tah hee	54	McD
Pvt. Stop Storekeeper	25	McD
Pvt. James Storekeeper	26	D

Name	Age	Company
Pvt. Tom Su ate	29	McD
Pvt. Sul la tee skie	20	E
Pvt. Sul te skie	20	E
Pvt. Tah ne yee sky Sunday	30	B
Sgt. William Sunday	30	McD
Pvt. Sun ne coo yoh	22	H
Pvt. Sun too le	18	E
Pvt. Sut tee cah Scontie	36	B
Pvt. Sut tu hah Joe	25	D
Pvt. Su Wah tie	30	G
Pvt. Su wa Kee	50	K
Pvt. Dick Su wa Kie	20	G
Pvt. Su wa Kie Ezekiel	45	I
Pvt. Su way Kie Wor Sortie	39	I
Sgt. Sweet Cow	56	D
Pvt. Sweet Water	20	C
Pvt. Swimmer (Creek)	26	E
Pvt. Swimmer	25	F
Pvt. Swimmer	19	H
Pvt. Alex Swimmer	34	E
Pvt. Jesse Swimmer	30	E
Pvt. Joe Swimmer	24	F
Pvt. Joseph Swimmer	19	K
Pvt. Ool skewe ney Swimmer	28	I
Pvt. Rider Swimmer	18	K
Pvt. Lewis Tabb	—	F
Pvt. David Tadpole	22	I
Sgt. Ely Tadpole	29	I
Pvt. John Tadpole	18	I
Sgt. Joshua Tadpole	34	I
Pvt. Daniel Tae lus Kie	32	H
Pvt. Tah cah Soh Kah Tee Ke chee	30	B
Pvt. Tah chur see Jack	22	G
Pvt. Tah chur see Tah lah	30	G
Pvt. Tah gah che gee Sy	22	McD
Pvt. Tah Ker yer oo cha loo ty	40	D
Sgt. Tah ker yer Wolf	37	D
Pvt. Tah law se Redbird	22	H

Name	Age	Company
Pvt. Tah le eus Ky Scraper	23	E
Pvt. Tah ne nah la	23	E
Pvt. David Tah ne noli	19	G
Pvt. Tah ne no li sken tah ee	40	G
Pvt. Sequoyah Tah le yeskie	30	K
Cpl. Tah ner yes ky	50	A
Pvt. Tah ne yes Kie	29	C
Sgt. Tah nie Walkingstick	60	E
Pvt. Tah Nowie Squirrel	30	G
Cpl. Tah yes Ky	49	A
Pvt. Tah yool Sin ee	18	D
Pvt. Ta Ke Na Se Nee	23	A
Pvt. Jim Tallow	25	McD
Pvt. Tallow Mays	26	H
Pvt. Sam Ta looke	67	C
Pvt. Tan chu lae ner	50	H
Farrier Tanner	50	D
Pvt. Aaron Tanner	27	D
Pvt. Jack Tanner	30	D
Pvt. Sequouah Tanner	30	D
Pvt. Tanner Clow yer Kee	23	D
Cpl. Tar che che Nick	44	G
Pvt. Tar los se	33	C
Sgt. Tarrapin Striker	60	F
Pvt. Tassel	22	C
Pvt. Tassel ah hur Mah	24	B
Pvt. Bill Taylor	24	McD
Pvt. Jim Taylor	17	McD
Pvt. John Taylor	32	McD
Pvt. Teacher	20	F
Pvt. Teacher Smith	38	F
Pvt. Te cah noo le Cloud	20	B
Pvt. Te cul Kel	32	C
Pvt. Tee cah nee ye skie	25	E
Pvt. Tee ca tos Kee	35	D
Pvt. Charles Tee hee	27	B
Pvt. Tee hur nee skie Tah lie Stay skie	30	I
Pvt. Tee Ker ne ye sky	21	A

Name	Age	Company
Pvt. Tee kin ee Mouse	51	D
Pvt. Tee lah ski ske Stop	50	G
Pvt. Tee lah ski ske Tar che chee	32	G
Pvt. Tee lah ski ske Twister	38	G
Pvt. Tee Sah skie	30	F
Pvt. Musk Mellon Tee sah tai skie	20	G
Pvt. Tee Say skie	40	B
Pvt. Tee see yor kee	25	McD
Pvt. Tee Ser ne he	36	A
Pvt. Bill Tee soo yoh	27	G
Pvt. Allick Tee tah Nur Sne	–	G
Pvt. Joseph Te Kah tos Kee	29	A
Pvt. Te Ke che Ah hur Nah	38	G
Sgt. Nelson Terapin	33	G
Cpl. Ter Nah ee	60	D
Pvt. Te sar Tah ske	40	D
Pvt. Tet yer ner skie	25	E
Pvt. Jeremiah Theodore	19	G
Pvt. Thirsty Tyger	30	D
Pvt. Thomas	20	G
Pvt. Thomas (Creek)	35	K
Cpl. Ticke Eater	33	I
Pvt. Ti e skie	30	H
Pvt. Tie ye skie	38	D
Pvt. Tie yes kie	37	McD
Pvt. Ned Timpson	28	H
Bugler Tle yer ker	19	D
Pvt. James Tobaco Will	31	K
Pvt. Tlos tah ner	29	E
Pvt. Tlo yer ker	50	A
Cpl. To cher la ner	40	A
Pvt. Tom	20	A
Pvt. Tom	25	D
Pvt. To nah yoh	36	McD
Pvt. Ton a tae ton e	18	H
Sgt. George Tony	35	C
Pvt. Too che	30	H

Name	Age	Company
Pvt. Too lees tee	55	D
Pvt. Too nah wee	40	G
Pvt. Too nie	30	C
Pvt. George Toonie	20	B
Pvt. Too nie ah	26	C
Pvt. Too nie William	22	G
Pvt. Ned Too quah tah	35	McD
Pvt. Too Se wae e tah	30	A
Pvt. Too woh nae ner too quar lah	25	G
Pvt. Tor chu lay nah	40	B
Pvt. Tor yeu nee see	26	McD
Sgt. John Towie	30	A
Pvt. John Towie	20	D
Pvt. Loo ney Townsend	18	A
Pvt. Toy ah tee see chee wa looke	26	B
Pvt. To ye ne Sie	27	E
Pvt. Tracker	65	F
Pvt. David Tracking Wolf	22	G
Pvt. William Triplett	19	B
Lt. Trotting Wolfe (Wolf)	29	K
Pvt. David Tucker	48	McD
Pvt. Jerry Tucker	45	H
Smith John Tucker	46	B
Pvt. Levi Tucker	22	McD
Pvt. Tuck se	40	H
Pvt. James Tun Suy lee	18	B
Pvt. Tur nee see Johnson	25	I
Pvt. Tur ne nall le	30	McD
Pvt. Tur noh wai lah ne	21	G
Pvt. Davis Turnover	20	D
Pvt. Isaac Turn Over	27	D
Pvt. Turnover Ty es kie	40	I
Pvt. Twister	40	C
Pvt. James Tyeall	22	McD
Pvt. Tyer	36	McD
Pvt. Tyer Mouse	30	D
Sgt. Wheeler Tyger	40	D

Name	Age	Company
Pvt. Ulla teesky	30	K
Pvt. Ul tee ske (Ulteesky)	33	H
Later a lieutenant		
Pvt. Ur tah ol tah	48	McD
Pvt. Ut tah woh ski Scontie	17	B
Pvt. Ave (Avery) Vann	27	H
Pvt. Clemm Vann	24	K
Capt. James Vann	39	E
Adj. James S. Vann	39	Staff
Pvt. Jesse Vann	26	E
Pvt. Jesse Vann	19	F
Cpl. Joseph Vann	40	K
Pvt. Josiah Vann	27	K
Pvt. Spirit Vann	18	K
Pvt. Saturday Vann	33	A
Quartermaster Israel G. Vore	40	Staff
Pvt. John Wagoner	25	E
Pvt. Wah he yus ke Blanket	25	H
Pvt. Wah Jah gee	19	K
Pvt. William Wah tar too Kar	31	McD
Pvt. Wahtie	25	A
Pvt. Walker	30	A
Pvt. Edmond Walker	28	B
Pvt. George Walker	22	F
Pvt. John Walker	47	F
Pvt. William Walker	16	H
Pvt. Walker Ground Squirrel	20	G
Pvt. John Walkingstick	20	E
Sgt. Levi Walkingstick	28	E
Pvt. Walking Wolf	30	K
Pvt. Walnut	33	F
Pvt. Washington	20	H
Pvt. Water falling	20	I
Pvt. Water Killer	44	C
Pvt. Watt	24	E
Pvt. Charles Watts	20	B
Pvt. Johnson Watts	44	C
Cpl. Peach Watts	35	B

Name	Age	Company
Sgt. Thomas Watts	35	C
Pvt. Walter Watts	36	B
Pvt. Watty (notchie Creek)	60	B
Lt. William Webber	45	F
Pvt. Weedy Field	23	K
Lt. White Catcher	46	B
Pvt. Davisson Whitekiller	31	G
Pvt. Steney Whitekiller	26	G
Pvt. Isaac Whitepath	22	C
Pvt. White Water	30	C
Pvt. Wild Cat Weeley	50	B
Pvt. Wild Cat yahola	28	K
Pvt. Wild Hog	21	B
Pvt. William Sour John	46	I
Pvt. Wilson	25	A
Pvt. Wilson	16	E
Cpl. David Wind	40	H
Pvt. Wind Chockram	20	A
Pvt. Nelson Wolf	—	D
Pvt. James Wolfe	44	E
Pvt. Wolftracker	52	A
Pvt. Woman Killer	20	I
Pvt. George Woodall	19	McD
Pvt. Osceola Woodall	31	McD
Pvt. Stephen Wool	20	E
Pvt. WorSaw tie	36	D
Pvt. Writer	23	D
Pvt. Yah hoo lah	19	A
Pvt. Yah nah Oola san tah	20	E
Pvt. James Ya ho la	25	K
Pvt. Sampson Yahola	30	K
Pvt. Thomas Yahola	27	K
Pvt. Yahola Sr	50	K
Pvt. Yal Sutch ee	20	D
Pvt. Reader Yellow	23	I
Pvt. Su wa key Yellowhammer	22	G
Sgt. Yellow Jacker	49	F
Pvt. Lewis Yorter	18	A

Name	Age	Company
Pvt. Charles Young	20	H
Lt. John Young	45	F
Pvt. John Young Jr.	18	F
Pvt. Josiah Young	20	F
Pvt. Thomas Young	30	F
Pvt. William Young	24	F
Pvt. Young Beaver	23	C
Pvt. Young Beaver	19	D
Pvt. Young Bird	24	D
Pvt. Young Bird	25	E
Pvt. Young Bird	30	K
Pvt. Issac Youngbird	22	G
Pvt. Youngbird Tah nowie	40	I
Pvt. Young Deer	25	A
Pvt. Young Deer	55	McD
Pvt. Young Duck	48	A
Pvt. Young Duck	48	McD
Pvt. Robin Young Duck	18	G
Pvt. Young Pig	43	McD
Pvt. Young Pigeon	27	A
Pvt. Young Puppy	43	B
Pvt. Young Squirrel	30	F
Pvt. Young Squirrel Flopper	30	I
Pvt. Young Tassel	22	McD
Pvt. Young Terrapin	30	K
Pvt. Young Wolf	27	D
Pvt. Young Wolfe	31	A
Pvt. Young Wolfe	31	H

Source: Compiled Service Records of Confederate Soldiers Who Served in Organizations Raised Directly by the Confederate Government, Microcopy 258, Rolls 77 and 78, National Archives Publications, Washington, D.C.

Bibliography

MANUSCRIPTS

National Archives Microfilm Publications, Washington, D.C.
  Compiled Service Records of Confederate Soldiers Who Served in Organizations Raised Directly by the Confederate Government. Microcopy 258, rolls 77 and 78.
  Compiled Records Showing Service of Military Units in Volunteer Union Organizations. Microcopy 594, roll 225.
  Compiled Records Showing Service of Military Units in Confederate Organizations. Microcopy 861, roll 74.
Northeastern State University, Tahlequah, Oklahoma
  Andrew Nave Letters.
  John Ross Papers.
Oklahoma Historical Society, Oklahoma City
  Grant Foreman Collection (John Ross Papers), Box 8.
  Grant Foreman Papers, Vol. 109.
  "History of the Service and List of Individuals of the Five Civilized Tribes in the Confederate Army Compiled from the Confederate Records in the Office of the Adjutant-General Under the Direction of Grant Foreman." Typescript. Vol. I. Washington, D.C. 1928.
  Indian Pioneer History.
  Shirk, Col. George H. "Civil War in Indian Territory: One Hundred Years Ago in Indian Territory." Typescript.
Pea Ridge National Military Park, Pea Ridge, Arkansas
  Bearss, Edwin C. "The Indians at Pea Ridge." Typescript.
Thomas Gilcrease Institute of American History and Art, Tulsa, Oklahoma
  John Drew Papers.
  Grant Foreman Papers. Vol. 39, Box 23, and Vol. 97, Box 43.
  John Ross Papers (61 and 62 series).
  William P. Ross Papers.
University of Oklahoma, Western History Collections, Norman

Cherokee Nation Papers.
William P. Ross Collection.
University of Tulsa
Alice Robertson Collection, dated letters.

GOVERNMENT DOCUMENTS

Adjutant General of the State of Kansas. *Report of the Adjutant General of the State of Kansas: 1861–1865.* Vol. I. Topeka, 1896.

Commissioner of Indian Affairs. *Report of the Commissioner of Indian Affairs. 1862–66.* Washington, D.C., 1863–66.

Delegates of the Cherokee Nation. *Communication of the Delegates of the Cherokee Nation to the President of the United States, Submitting the Memorial of Their National Council, with the Correspondence Between John Ross, Principal Chief, and Certain Officers of the Rebellious States.* Washington, D.C., 1866.

————. *Memorial of the Delegates of the Cherokee Nation to the President of the United States and the Senate and House of Representatives in Congress.* Washington, D.C., 1866.

————. *Reply of the Delegates of the Cherokee Nation to the Pamphlet of the Commissioner of Indian Affairs.* Washington, D.C., 1866.

Joint Committee on the Conduct of the War. *Report of the Joint Committee on the Conduct of the War.* 37th Cong., 3d Sess., Senate Rep. Comm. No. 108. Washington, D.C., 1863.

Pike, Albert. *Message of the President and Report of Albert Pike: Commissioner of the Confederate States to the Indian Nations West of Arkansas, of the Results of His Mission.* Richmond, 1861.

Usher, J. P. *Letter from J. P. Usher, Assistant Secretary of the Interior in Answer to Resolution of the House of 28th Ultimo Relative to Mode and Amount of Relief Extended to Indian Refugees in Southern Kansas.* 37th Cong., 7th Sess., House of Representatives, Executive Document 132, Washington, D.C., 1862.

The War of the Rebellion: A Compilation of the Official Records of the Union and Confederate Armies. 130 vols. Washington, D.C., 1880–1901.

NEWSPAPERS

Arkansas Gazette (Little Rock), 1861 and 1862.
Clarksville *Standard* (Texas), 1861.
New York *Times,* 1861 and 1862.
Texas Republican (Washington, Texas), 1861 and 1862.
Washington *Telegraph* (Arkansas), 1862.

BOOKS

Abel, Annie Heloise. *The American Indian as Participant in the Civil War*. Cleveland, 1919.

———. *The American Indian as Slaveholder and Secessionist*. Cleveland, 1915.

———. *The American Indian Under Reconstruction*. Cleveland, 1925.

Abott, John Stevens. *The History of the Civil War in America*. Springfield, Mass., 1866.

Agnew, Brad. *Fort Gibson: Terminal of the Trail of Tears*. Norman, 1980.

Allsopp, Fred W. *The Life Story of Albert Pike*. Little Rock, 1920.

Anderson, Ephraim McD. *Memoirs of the First Missouri Brigade*. St. Louis, 1868.

Anderson, Mabel W. *Life of General Stand Watie*. N.p., n.d.

Bailey, Minie Thomas. *Reconstruction in Indian Territory: A Story of Avarice, Discrimination, and Opportunism*. Port Washington, N.Y., 1972.

Ballenger, T. L. *Around Tahlequah Council Fires*. Muskogee, Okla., 1935.

Barron, Samuel Benton. *The Lone Star Defenders: A Chronicle of the Third Texas Cavalry, Ross' Brigade*. New York, 1908.

Bearss, Edwin C., and Arrell M. Gibson. *Fort Smith: Little Gibralter on the Arkansas*. Norman, 1969.

Bevier, R. S. *History of the First and Second Missouri Confederate Brigades, 1861–1862*. St. Louis, 1879.

Blake, William O. *Pictorial History of the Great Rebellion*. Columbus, Ohio, 1866.

Britton, Wiley. *The Civil War on the Border, 1861–1862*. New York, 1890.

———. *Memoirs of the Rebellion on the Border*. Chicago, 1882.

———. *The Union Indian Brigade in the Civil War*. Kansas City, 1922.

Cantrell, M. L., and Mac Harris, eds. *Kepis and Turkey Calls: An Anthology of the War Between the States in Indian Territory*. Oklahoma City, 1982.

Castel, Albert. *A Frontier State at War: Kansas, 1861–65*. Ithaca, 1958.

———. *General Sterling Price and the Civil War in the West*. Baton Rouge, 1968.

Catton, Bruce. *Terrible Swift Sword*. New York, 1963.

The Century Civil War Book: The Famous History of the Civil War by People Who Actually Fought It. New York, 1978.

Cooper, Dennis, ed. *Cherokee Almanac, 1861*. Rpr. Muskogee, Okla., 1972.

Dale, Edward Everett, and Gaston Litton, eds. *Cherokee Cavaliers: Forty Years of Cherokee History as Told in the Correspondence of the Ridge-Watie-Boudinot Family*. Norman, 1939.

Debo, Angie. *The Road to Disappearance: A History of the Creek Indians*. Norman, 1979.

Duncan, Robert Lipscomb. *Reluctant General: The Life and Times of Albert Pike*. New York, 1961.

Eaton, Rachael Caroline. *John Ross and the Cherokee Indians*. Menasha, Wisc., 1914.

Evans, Gen. Clement A., ed. *Confederate Military History*. Vols. X and XI. Secaucus, N.J., n.d.

Faulk, Odie B., Kenny A. Franks, and Paul F. Lambert, eds. *Early Military Forts and Posts in Oklahoma*. Oklahoma City, 1978.

Fisher, LeRoy H., ed. *Civil War Battles in the West*. Manhattan, Kan., 1981.

Foreman, Carolyn Thomas. *Park Hill*. Muskogee, Okla., 1948.

Foreman, Grant. *Fort Gibson: A Brief History*. Muskogee, Okla., n.d.

———. *A History of Oklahoma*. Norman, 1945.

———. *Indian Removal*. Norman, 1976.

———. *Marcy and the Gold Seekers*. Norman, 1968.

Franks, Kenny A. *Stand Watie and the Agony of the Cherokee Nation*. Memphis, 1979.

Gibson, Arrell M. *The Chickasaws*. Norman, 1971.

Guernsey, Alfred H., and Henry M. Alden. *Harper's Pictorial History of the Civil War*. Chicago, 1866.

Harlow, Victor E., and Arrell M. Gibson. *Harlow's Oklahoma History*. Norman, 1967.

Hartje, Robert G. *Van Dorn: The Life and Times of a Confederate General*. Nashville, 1967.

Ingersoll, Lurton Dunham. *Iowa and the Rebellion*. Philadelphia, 1866.

James, Marquis. *The Life of Andrew Jackson*. Indianapolis, 1938.

Jordan, H. Glenn, and Thomas M. Holmes, eds. *Indian Leaders: Oklahoma's First Statesmen*. Oklahoma City, 1979.

Lackey, Vinson. *The Forts of Oklahoma*. Tulsa, 1963.

McReynolds, Edwin C. *Missouri: A History of the Crossroads State*. Norman, 1975.

Miller, Francis Trevelyan, ed. *The Photographic History of the Civil War.*
10 vols. New York, 1957.

Monaghan, Jay. *Civil War on the Western Border, 1854–1865.* Boston,
1955.

Mooney, James. *Historical Sketch of the Cherokee.* Chicago, 1975.

Morris, John W., and Edwin C. McReynolds. *Historical Atlas of
Oklahoma.* Norman, 1965.

Morrison, William Brown. *Military Posts and Camps in Oklahoma.*
Oklahoma City, 1936.

Moulton, Gary E. *John Ross, Cherokee Chief.* Athens, Ga., 1978.

——, ed. *The Papers of Chief John Ross.* Vol. II: *1840–1866.* Norman,
1985.

Pea Ridge National Military Park, Arkansas. Washington, D.C., 1971.

Rampp, Larry C., and Donald L. Rampp. *The Civil War in the Indian
Territory.* Austin, 1975.

Rose, Victor M. *The Life and Service of General Ben McCulloch.* Philadelphia, 1888.

——. *Ross' Texas Brigade.* Kennesaw, Ga., 1960.

Ross, John. *Message of the Principal Chief of Cherokee Nation Together
with the Declaration of the Cherokee People of the Cause Which Have Led
Them to Withdraw from Their Connection to the U. States.* 1861; rpr.
Washington, D.C., 1943.

Ross, Mrs. William P., ed. *The Life and Times of Hon. William P. Ross.*
Ft. Smith, Ark., 1893.

Ruskin, Gertrude McDavis. *John Ross: Chief of an Eagle Race.* Decatur,
Ga., 1963.

Staff of Pea Ridge National Military Park. *The Battle of Pea Ridge.* N.p.,
n.d.

Starr, Emitt. *History of the Cherokee Indians and Their Legends and
Folklore.* Oklahoma City, 1921.

Stuart, Captain A. A. *Iowa Colonels and Regiments: Being a History of
Iowa Regiments in the War of the Rebellion.* Des Moines, 1865.

Wardell, Morris L. *A Political History of the Cherokee Nation, 1838–
1907.* Norman, 1977.

Wilder, Daniel W. *The Annals of Kansas.* Topeka, 1875.

Wiley, Bell Irvin. *The Life of Johnny Reb: The Common Soldier of the
Confederacy.* Indianapolis, 1943.

Woodruff, William E. *With Light Guns.* Little Rock, 1903.

Woodward, Grace Steele. *The Cherokees.* Norman, 1963.

Wright, Marcus J. *Arkansas in the War, 1861–1865*. Batesville, Ark., 1963.

Wright, Marcus J., and Harold B. Simpson. *Texas in the War, 1861–1865*. Hillsboro, Tex., 1965.

Wright, Muriel H., George H. Shirk, and Kenny A. Franks. *Mark of Heritage*. Norman, 1976.

ARTICLES

Abel, Annie Heloise. "The Indian in the Civil War." *American Historical Review*, XV (January, 1910), 281–96.

Ballenger, T. L. "The Death and Burial of Major Ridge." *Chronicles of Oklahoma*, LI (Spring, 1973), 100–105.

———. "The Keetoowahs and Their Dances." *Chronicles of Oklahoma*, LXI (Summer, 1983), 194–99.

Bearss, Edwin C. "The Battle of Pea Ridge." *Arkansas Historical Quarterly*, XX (Spring, 1961), 74–94.

———. "The Civil War Comes to Indian Territory, 1861: The Flight of Opothleyahola." *Journal of the West*, XI (January, 1972), 9–42.

———. "The First Day at Pea Ridge, March 7, 1862." *Arkansas Historical Quarterly*, XVII (Summer, 1958), 132–54.

———. "From Rolla to Fayetteville with General Curtis." *Arkansas Historical Quarterly*, XIX (Autumn, 1960), 225–59.

Blunt, James G. "General Blunt's Account of His Civil War Experience." *Kansas Historical Quarterly*, I (May, 1932), 211–65.

Britton, Wiley. "Some Reminiscences of the Cherokee People." *Chronicles of Oklahoma*, V (March, 1927), 180–84.

Broemeling, Carol B. "Cherokee Indian Agents, 1830–1874." *Chronicles of Oklahoma*, L (Winter, 1972–73), 458–73.

Brown, John P. "Eastern Cherokee Chiefs." *Chronicles of Oklahoma*, XVI (March, 1938), 3–35.

Brown, Walter L. "Pea Ridge: Gettysburg of the West." *Arkansas Historical Quarterly*, XV (Spring, 1956), 3–16.

———. "Rowing Against the Stream: The Case of Albert Pike from National Whig to Secessionist." *Arkansas Historical Quarterly*, XXXIX (Autumn, 1980), 230–46.

Burch, Paul W. "Kansas: Bushwackers vs. Jayhawkers." *Journal of the West*, XIV (January, 1975), 83–104.

Castel, Albert. "A New View of the Battle of Pea Ridge." *Missouri Historical Review*, LXII (January, 1968), 136–51.

Clifford, Roy A. "The Indian Regiments in the Battle of Pea Ridge." *Chronicles of Oklahoma*, XXV (Winter, 1947–48), 314–22.

Cory, Charles E. "The Sixth Kansas Cavalry and Its Commander." In *Collections of the Kansas State Historical Society, 1909–1910*, XI, 217–37. Topeka, 1910.

Curtis, Brig. Gen. Samuel R. "Composition and Losses of the Union Army"; and Van Dorn, Major-General Earl. "Composition and Losses of the Confederate Army." In R. V. Johnson and C. C. Buel, eds., *Battles and Leaders of the Civil War*, I, 337. 4 vols. 1884–88; rpr. New York, 1956.

Dale, Edward Everett. "The Cherokees in the Confederacy." *Journal of Southern History*, XIII (May, 1947), 160–85.

——. "Some Letters of General Stand Watie." *Chronicles of Oklahoma*, I (January, 1921), 30–59.

Danziger, Edmund. "The Office of Indian Affairs and the Problem of Civil War Refugees in Kansas." *Kansas Historical Quarterly*, XXXV (Autumn, 1969), 267–75.

Debo, Angie. "The Location of the Battle of Round Mountains." *Chronicles of Oklahoma*, XLI (Spring, 1963), 70–104.

——. "Southern Refugees of the Cherokee Nation." *Southwestern Historical Quarterly*, XXXV (April, 1932), 255–66.

Downey, Fairfax. "The Blue, the Grey, and the Red." *Civil War Times Illustrated*, I (July, 1962), 6–9, 26–30.

DuChateau, Andre Paul. "The Creek Nation on the Eve of the Civil War." *Chronicles of Oklahoma*, LII (Fall, 1974), 290–315.

Edwards, Dale. "Arkansas: Pea Ridge and State Division." *Journal of the West*, XIV (January, 1975), 167–84.

Finley, Linda. "Notes from the Diary of Susan E. Foreman." *Chronicles of Oklahoma*, XLVIII (Winter, 1969–70), 388–97.

Fisher, LeRoy, and Jerry Gill. "Confederate Indian Forces Outside of Indian Territory." *Chronicles of Oklahoma*, XLVI (Autumn, 1968), 249–84.

Fisher, LeRoy, and Kenny A. Franks. "Confederate Victory at Chusto-Talasah." *Chronicles of Oklahoma*, XLIX (Winter, 1971–72), 452–76.

Foreman, Carolyn Thomas. "The Coodey Family of Indian Territory." *Chronicles of Oklahoma*, XXV (Winter, 1947–48), 323–41.

——. "Early History of Webbers Falls." *Chronicles of Oklahoma*, XXIX (Winter, 1951–52), 441–83.

———. "Israel G. Vore and Levering Manual Labor School." *Chronicles of Oklahoma*, XXV (Autumn, 1947), 198–217.

———. "Joseph Absalom Scales." *Chronicles of Oklahoma*, XXVIII (Winter, 1950–51), 418–32.

Foreman, Grant. "The Murder of Elias Boudinot." *Chronicles of Oklahoma*, XII (March, 1934), 19–24.

———. "Reminiscences of Mr. R. P. Vann, East of Webbers Falls, Oklahoma." *Chronicles of Oklahoma*, XI (June, 1933), 838–44.

Franks, Kenny A. "Confederate Treaties with the Five Civilized Tribes." *Chronicles of Oklahoma*, L (Winter, 1972–73), 458–73.

Gaines, W. Craig. "The Cherokee Nation in the Civil War." *Loyal Legion Historical Journal*, XXX (February, 1974), 8–11.

Hartje, Robert G. "A Confederate Dilemma Across the Mississippi." *Arkansas Historical Quarterly*, XVII (Summer, 1958), 130–31.

Heath, Gary N. "The First Federal Invasion of Indian Territory." *Chronicles of Oklahoma*, XLIV (Winter, 1966–67), 409–19.

Hicks, Hanna. "The Diary of Hanna Hicks." *American Scene*, XIII, No. 3 (1972), entire issue.

Holman, Tom. "William G. Coffin, Lincoln's Superintendent of Indian Affairs for the Southern Superintendency." *Kansas Historical Quarterly*, XXXIX (Winter, 1973), 491–514.

Lemley, Harry J. "Historic Letters of General Ben McCulloch and Chief John Ross in the Civil War." *Chronicles of Oklahoma*, XL (Autumn, 1962), 286–94.

McFadden, Marguerite. "The Saga of 'Rich Joe' Vann." *Chronicles of Oklahoma*, LXI (Spring, 1983), 68–79.

McNeal, Kenneth. "Confederate Treaties with the Tribes of Indian Territory." *Chronicles of Oklahoma*, XLII (Winter, 1964–65), 408–20.

Meserve, John Bartlett. "Chief John Ross." *Chronicles of Oklahoma*, XIII (December, 1935), 421–37.

———. "Chief Lewis Downing and Chief Charles Thompson (Oochalata)." *Chronicles of Oklahoma*, XVI (September, 1938), 315–25.

———. "Chief Opothleyahola." *Chronicles of Oklahoma*, IX (December, 1931), 445–53.

———. "Chief William Potter Ross." *Chronicles of Oklahoma*, XV (March, 1938), 21–29.

———. "The MacIntoshes." *Chronicles of Oklahoma*, X (Summer, 1932), 310–25.

Mooney, James. "Myths of the Cherokee." In *Nineteenth Annual Re-*

port of the Bureau of American Ethnology to the Secretary of the Smithsonian Institution, 1897–98. Part I, pp. 3–548. Washington, D.C., 1900.

Morton, Ohland. "Confederate Government Relations with the Five Civilized Tribes." *Chronicles of Oklahoma*, XXXI (Summer, 1953), 189–204, and (Autumn, 1953), 299–322.

Moulton, Gary E. "John Ross and W. P. Dole: A Case Study of Lincoln's Indian Policy." *Journal of the West*, XII (July, 1977), 414–23.

Royce, Charles C. "The Cherokee Nation of Indians." In *Fifth Annual Report of the Bureau of Ethnology to the Secretary of the Smithsonian Institution*, pp. 121–378. Washington, D.C., 1887.

Shirk, George H. "The Place of Indian Territory in the Command Structure of the Civil War." *Chronicles of Oklahoma*, XLV (Winter, 1967–68), 464–71.

Shoemaker, Arthur. "The Battle of Chustenahlah." *Chronicles of Oklahoma*, XXXVIII (Summer, 1960), 180–84.

Thoburn, Joseph, ed. "The Cherokee Question." *Chronicles of Oklahoma*, II (March, 1924), 141–252.

Trickett, Dean. "The Civil War in the Indian Territory, 1861." *Chronicles of Oklahoma*, XVIII (September, 1940), 266–80.

———. "The Civil War in the Indian Territory, 1862." *Chronicles of Oklahoma*, XIX (December, 1941), 381–96.

Ware, James W. "Indian Territory." *Journal of the West*, XVI (April, 1977), 101–13.

Whitman, Louise. "Recent Activities of the Tulsa Historical Society." *Chronicles of Oklahoma*, XXI (March, 1943), 64–70.

Wright, Muriel H. "Colonel Cooper's Civil War Report on the Battle of Round Mountain." *Chronicles of Oklahoma*, XXXIX (Winter, 1961–62), 352–97.

———. "Notes on the Life of Mrs. Hannah Worchester Hicks Hitchcock and the Park Hill Press." *Chronicles of Oklahoma*, XIX (December, 1941), 348–55.

Wright, Muriel H., and LeRoy H. Fischer. "Civil War Sites in Oklahoma." *Chronicles of Oklahoma*, XLIV (Summer, 1966), 282–314.

THESES

Bahos, Charles Lee. "John Ross: Unionist or Secessionist in 1861?" Master's thesis, University of Tulsa, 1968.

Heard, Edward F. "Dwight Mission Under the American Board."
Master's thesis, University of Tulsa, 1958.
Tyner, Howard Q. "The Keetoowah Society in Cherokee History."
Master's thesis, University of Tulsa, 1949.

Index